J. W. Rogerson is Emeritus Professor of
of Sheffield and Canon Emeritus of ᴖᴜᴄᴜᴜᴄᴜ ᴄᴜᴜᴄᴜᴜ ᴜᴜ
main books include *Myth in Old Testament Interpretation* (1974),
*Old Testament Criticism in the Nineteenth Century: England
and Germany* (1984), *W. M. L. de Wette, Founder of Modern
Biblical Criticism: An Intellectual Biography* (1992), *The Bible
and Criticism in Victorian Britain: Profiles of F. D. Maurice and
William Robertson Smith* (1995), *An Introduction to the Bible*
(1999, 2nd ed. 2005, 3rd ed. 2011), *Theory and Practice in
Old Testament Ethics* (2004) and *A Theology of the Old Testament:
Cultural Memory, Communication and Being Human* (SPCK,
2009). He also edited *The Oxford Illustrated History of the Bible*
(2001) and (with Judith M. Lieu) *The Oxford Handbook of
Biblical Studies* (2006).

THE ART OF BIBLICAL PRAYER

J. W. Rogerson

First published in Great Britain in 2011

Society for Promoting Christian Knowledge
36 Causton Street
London SW1P 4ST
www.spckpublishing.co.uk

British Library Cataloguing-in-Publication Data
A catalogue record for this book is available from the British Library

ISBN 978–0–281–06450–2

1 3 5 7 9 10 8 6 4 2

Typeset by Graphicraft Ltd, Hong Kong
Printed in Great Britain by MPG Books Group

Produced on paper from sustainable forests

For Ellie

Contents

———•◦•———

Introduction

A biblical scholar is not the best-qualified person to write on the subject of prayer. I have ventured to do so for two reasons. First, as a result of a call by the Bishop of Sheffield for the churches of his diocese to hold special prayers during the period from Ascension to Whitsun 2010, I have preached, and continue to preach, a series of sermons on prayer and the Lord's Prayer at Beauchief Abbey. I wanted the congregation to be able to read the substance of what I have said in these sermons. Because the material in the chapters has originated in sermons, a popular form of address will be found in some sections.

Second, although I pray almost every day, I do not regard myself as particularly good at prayer (whatever 'good' means in this context). When I read books about prayer by experts, I feel that they belong to a different world from me. I feel that there is a need for a book about prayer by someone who is not very good at it. Perhaps such a book will help others who are not very good at it. I have also tried to deal honestly with questions that arise from the theory and practice of prayer. If there are aspects of inadequate coverage (for example, I have not dealt with worship as a separate subject), that must be put down to my inadequate grasp of the subject. At the very least, my friends in the congregation at Beauchief Abbey will have the opportunity to read and reflect on what I have said over several months.

Miss Mary Hodge has read a draft of the book and has made many helpful comments and suggestions. I am most grateful to her.

1

What is prayer?

————•◦•————

'Prayer' is a word that is used in a number of different ways. For many people it means essentially petition or intercession. When we say, 'I'll remember you in my prayers,' we mean something like, 'I'll ask God to bless/heal/support you.' Understood in this way, prayer easily becomes an 'extra' – something that is not essential to Christianity, but something that some Christians do sometimes, as the need arises, when they are not in church. Later on in this book there will be a chapter on intercessory or petitionary prayer; but for the moment it will be argued that prayer should be understood as inseparable from Christianity in the sense that to practise Christianity is to practise prayer and vice versa. How can this be?

In his *Reality and Prayer*, J. B. Magee writes that 'prayer is a gift of God and a work of his grace'.[1] This quotation will be the driving force behind much that follows in these pages. In the first place it puts a question-mark against the idea that prayer is primarily petition or intercession. In these latter activities it is *we* who take the initiative in bringing our concerns before God, not God who gives us something through which grace is worked. The way in which I want to spell out how prayer can be thought of as a divine gift is by comparing it with a special language.

I do not have in mind a foreign language, but the language that has to be learned if a person is to become a specialist in

———
[1] J. B. Magee, *Reality and Prayer*, London: Hodder and Stoughton, 1958, p. 40.

1

a particular trade, profession or creative sphere. My father, who studied at night school to become a carpenter and joiner, and for whom I spent many hours as a boy holding, fetching and carrying items, taught me terms such as architrave (the moulded rectangular frame round a door or window), nogging (brickwork set within a frame) and tenon (a protruding piece of wood to be inserted into a mortice, a mortice being a specially cut cavity). A niece of mine who is studying dentistry uses a formidable array of technical terms in her written course work.

It is important to stress here that I am not talking about something that is intellectual and elitist. Unfortunately, when it comes to Christian faith, there seems to be a presumption in the Church not only that it would be too much to expect 'ordinary people' to master any distinctive concepts fundamental to Christianity, but also that this would be undesirable in principle. It is true that while Dietrich Bonhoeffer was detained by the Nazis in prison in 1944, he wrestled with the question of whether it was possible to formulate a version of Christianity that did not require any distinctive theological concepts and thus a special type of Christian language; but it is doubtful whether this, if possible, would be any more likely to succeed than an interpretation of, say, Islam, that avoided any mention of the Qur'an, Muhammad or the pilgrimage to Mecca.[2] Bonhoeffer was probably criticizing 'religion' in the sense of a set of widely held beliefs deemed both inside and outside the churches to be an essential part of Christianity. I would

---

[2] See D. Bonhoeffer, *Widerstand und Ergebung: Briefe und Aufzeichnungen aus der Haft*, Munich: Kaiser Verlag, 1951, p. 179; ET *Letters and Papers from Prison*, London: SCM Press, 1953, pp. 122–3. Bonhoeffer considered the possibility of a non-theological interpretation of Christianity, which has often been (mis)represented in English as 'religionless Christianity'. See further the essays by P. Selby, 'Christianity in a World Come of Age' and G. B. Kelly, 'Prayer and Action for Justice: Bonhoeffer's Spirituality' in J. W. de Grouchy (ed.), *The Cambridge Companion to Dietrich Bonhoeffer*, Cambridge: Cambridge University Press, 1999, pp. 226–45 and 246–68.

agree with his criticisms. When I speak of a distinctive language of Christianity and prayer, I have something else in mind.

I have in mind a particular way of looking at the world. That way is best arrived at, in my opinion, by considering some of the best-known parables of Jesus. These are stories that are easily remembered and which express an understanding of the world that is challenging and inspiring. I begin with the parables of the Lost Sheep and the Lost Coin in Luke 15.1–10.[3] These 'Parables of Human Instinct', as Oliver Quick called them, set out from human feelings. We have all temporarily lost something at some time in our lives – keys, watches, mobile telephones, books – and we have had feelings of frustration and loss out of all proportion to the fact that we had *not* lost the overwhelmingly vast remainder of our possessions. Again, the joy and relief of finding a lost object, when we do so, is out of all proportion to its insignificance as a part of our possessions; yet we want to tell others that we have found what was lost, and want them to share our joy.

In the two parables exactly this same thing is described. The shepherd forgets that he has 99 sheep that are safely in his care, and goes after the one lost sheep because he feels somehow incomplete without it. He may even put the safety of the 99 at risk, but in such situations instinct can overrule calculation. When he finds the lost sheep he is overjoyed and calls on his friends and neighbours to share this joy. Precisely what the woman has lost is disputed by the commentators. Was it a coin from a kind of necklace that was her insurance against her husband divorcing her? Was it part of scarce savings? Was it a comparatively valueless object? It makes no difference to the parable. People can feel as incomplete and frustrated over the loss of a trivial item as over the loss of a valuable one. Whether

---

[3] The interpretation of these parables offered here is indebted to O. C. Quick, *The Realism of Christ's Parables*, London: SCM Press, 1937, pp. 29–32.

valuable or not, the lost item causes the woman to search exhaustively in the house, and when she finds the coin she calls on her friends and neighbours to rejoice with her. At the end of each story Jesus used these human emotions to describe what happens in heaven in connection with human behaviour. There is more joy in heaven (a possible way of saying 'God', observing Jewish conventions about treating the word 'God' with respect) over one sinner who repents than over 99 who do not need to do so. Similarly, in the case of the Lost Coin, there is joy among the angels of God over one sinner who repents. Quick draws out the implications of this memorably:

> 'You belong to God', he [Jesus] seems to say, 'you are in fact his property, his children. Can you suppose that men care more about their property and their own children than God cares about his? Can you believe that he implanted these instincts of ownership and parental affection in man's soul, and that they are not dim reflections of something infinitely more glorious in himself?'[4]

The realization that our best human instincts may also be a clue to God's concern for us may, for some, be a starting-point for Christian faith. It is certainly fundamental to the way of understanding the world that affects the language of prayer.

The parable of the Prodigal Son (Luke 15.11–32) is different from the two parables that precede it, in that some human instincts are shown not to be clues to the nature of God. The elder brother no doubt sums up what many people would instinctively do if they were in his position, and I have known people to be deeply offended by what they perceive, not unreasonably, to be the unfairness of the parable: that the wasteful, good-for-nothing son seems to finish up better off than the

---

[4] Quick, *Realism*, p. 34.

hard-working son who was loyal to his father. In actual fact the parable clearly marks out the difference between a world that is based on strict justice and what is deserved, and one that takes seriously the implications of repentance and forgiveness. The elder son represents justice and what is deserved, but cannot bring himself to forgive his brother. This inability to forgive would have been bad news for the prodigal if he had been met on his return not by his father but by his brother. Light is shed on the saying of Jesus that if we cannot forgive others, God cannot forgive us (see Matthew 6.14–15). The father's reaction in welcoming home his wayward son seems to create injustice and to overlook loyalty, but they are necessary if the prodigal is to become what he had ceased to be, namely a son in his father's house. Two theological technical terms are implicit in the father's treatment of the returning son: justification and sanctification. Justification in the parable means that the broken relationship between father and son has been restored, and restored by the undeserved mercy extended by the father to the son. Sanctification means that the son has returned to the one place where he can become a loyal son once more; where he can turn his back on the 'loose living' that had devoured his fortune, and be remade because of his father's mercy and love.

A fourth parable that is relevant to this chapter is that of the Labourers in the Vineyard (Matthew 20.1–16). Much light has been shed on this story by recent research into the social and economic background to the New Testament.[5] This has explained why the owner of the vineyard did not employ sufficient workers at the beginning of the day, but visited the market place on four occasions, the latest being one hour before the end of the working day. Workers engaged

---

[5] L. Schottroff, 'Die Güte Gottes und die Solidarität von Menschen: Das Gleichnis von den Arbeitern im Weinberg' in L. Schottroff, *Befreiungserfahrungen: Studien zur Sozialgeschichte des Neuen Testaments*, Munich: Kaiser Verlag, 1990, pp. 36–56.

later than the beginning of the day were entirely at the mercy of any employer as to what he would pay them (see Matthew 20.4). An unscrupulous employer could keep his wage bill down by employing few workers at the beginning of the day for the agreed daily wage, and more workers later in the day for much less than the daily rate. In the parable, the owner of the vineyard pays the agreed daily wage to all the workers, whether they worked for twelve hours or for one hour. This naturally causes resentment on the part of those who worked for twelve hours, but the employer seems to have been mindful of the fact that it cannot have been pleasant for men with dependants to support to have stood idle in the market place all day hoping that someone might give them work. The parable shows that in the kind of world in which we live, generosity that is intended to do something about the injustices that people suffer, will itself create injustice for anyone with no room for compassion.

A particular view of the world begins to emerge from a consideration of these parables. It is a world in which justice and what people strictly deserve have to be tempered by forgiveness, mercy and generosity. Where this is done, it becomes possible for people to find their way back from the many equivalents of the riotous living in the far country, to the welcome and healing of the father's house. It gives hope to people who would otherwise have no hope. The parables outline the alternative: the equivalent of the repentant son being turned away from the door; the exploited workers going back empty-handed to hungry families. But this world epitomized by hope and compassion is not simply one that could be thought of and endorsed by sensitive humanists; it appeals to human instincts to look beyond human hopes and aspirations to a divine order that itself can be thought of in terms of longings for restoration and wholeness. It is this fact that links this view of the world to prayer. Prayer can have many definitions, but whatever else it means, it is about uniting human hopes for a better world with the divine dimension to which the human experience of losing and finding points. It is within that union of human hope and divine reassurance that the special language of prayer emerges, and enables people to express their hopes and aspirations. Some of these special items of language have been mentioned. It is time to mention them again and to define them more closely. I shall discuss forgiveness, grace, mercy, repentance, justification and sanctification.

Forgiveness is not about forgetting the past; it is about handling the past creatively. An unforgiven past can become like a festering wound in the memory of an individual or group. It can enable the past to dominate the present and future as old grievances are continually given fresh life and enabled to nourish feelings of bitterness. Forgiveness is not a matter of forgetting about past wrongs of injustice. Where possible it is about putting them right. It may involve the admission that wrong was on both sides, not merely one side. Forgiveness is about overcoming evil with good. It is not about using the word 'sorry' as though it were a truce word whose mere utterance cancels out any responsibility there might be for the damaging of a relationship. Forgiveness is always the more difficult option. It is easier to let the past blight the present and future than to rob the past of its power to cast a shadow over the present. In the parable of the Prodigal Son, the elder brother is unable to forget the past; the father does not forget it either, but ensures that it does not prevent the returning son from beginning a new life.

Grace is a free gift offered by the giver without any intention or expectation that any obligation should thereby be created. If someone says to another, 'Because I have given you this and that, I expect you to be loyal to me and respect me,' then whatever else was being exercised in the giving, it was not grace. This can be illustrated by the elder brother in the parable. No doubt he had the right to expect his father's gratitude. But to the extent that he expected his father's gratitude, his service was not an act of grace even though it was undoubtedly praiseworthy. Grace therefore has about it an element of irrational and exorbitant generosity, but this is what gives it the potentiality to transform lives and situations.

Mercy is closely allied to grace and forgiveness in that it sees the limitation of justice in a world that is shot through with structural unfairness and the maintenance of double standards. The owner of the vineyard in the parable is merciful in the sense that he sees the limitations of the economic rules that apply to day labourers and the powerful advantage that these rules give to employers. He deliberately does not apply the rules. The mercy of God means, among other things, that God sees the shortcomings and dilemmas in terms of which people have to live out their lives and passes upon them a judgement that is sensitive to these factors.

Repentance is often wrongly understood in terms of the Greek word *metanoia*, which means to change one's mind, as opposed to the Hebrew concept of *t^eshuvah*, which means 'turning' or 'returning'. The Hebrew verb *shuv* is simple and graphic. It means 'turn' or 'return', the underlying idea being that someone is going along a false or dangerous path and needs to turn back or to turn onto a better path. It has to do with acting, not merely thinking. In the parable the prodigal certainly changed his mind; but more importantly, he retraced his steps and returned to his father's house. This was costly. There was not only the uncertainty of how his father or brother would react, but also the shame that he would feel when he met those who had known him. Suppose his father *had* made him one of his hired servants (cf. Luke 15.19)? If forgiveness and grace are costly, so is true repentance.

Justification is a word that comes in the letters of Paul (see Romans 3.26). It means that a person who in no way deserves to be accepted by God (the whole human race) is, against all the odds, in fact accepted. The word has legal overtones, and these have led to discussions about how guilty individuals can fulfil the just demands of God's laws and the penalties for breaking them. This, in turn, has led to theories about the death of Christ fulfilling the demands of the law on behalf of repentant sinners. The view taken here is that such an approach is hard to reconcile with the teaching of the parables discussed in this chapter. The father does not require anything to be made good or any penalty to be paid before he can welcome the returning prodigal as his son. Similarly, the parables about losing and finding point to a great longing on the part of God to accept those who repent. In the spirit of these parables, justification will be understood here as what happened when the father ran, embraced and kissed the returning prodigal. Against all the odds, a person who did not deserve to be accepted, was accepted.

Sanctification is another term from the letters of Paul (see 1 Corinthians 1.30), and refers to the process of becoming holy, in the sense of learning to live for God and for others rather than only for the self. In the parable of the Prodigal Son it is what we can presume happened to the prodigal once he had returned home. He was in the best situation to begin a new life of loyalty and service.

Some readers may be surprised at the terms that have been chosen for this description of the language of prayer. They may wonder what has happened to terms such as adoration, confession and praise. These are words that clearly have to do with prayer; but from the point of view that will be followed in this book they are secondary rather than primary terms. The terms that have been chosen and defined are intended to establish a framework or view of reality within which activities such as confession and adoration (which will be addressed in later chapters) are, or can be, carried out. This framework derives from the view of God that has been extracted from the parables that have been discussed. It is a framework that is different from a hard-nosed competitive world-view, where the weakest goes to the wall and 'knocking heads together' and 'tough management' are considered to be supreme virtues. This framework may also be different from some aspects of organized Christianity, such as the Church of England in its pageantry mode (by which I mean the pomp and ceremony of national and civic services and big diocesan occasions, all of which I find hard to reconcile with the simplicity of the ministry of Jesus as presented in the Gospels).

An important point now has to be made. Language implies a community of some kind, otherwise it has no communicative partners or purpose. Now it might be said that prayer is primarily communication with God, and that this can be done privately, and without the help or need of a community. While this is true, it is not the whole truth. Languages are learned from others. The same is true of prayer. The language which makes up the framework of prayer comes to us from others in various ways. Even if prayer is (inadequately in my view) understood exclusively as a private matter between an individual and God, this is possible only by the contribution of tradition and the work of others.

What this comes down to is that prayer is not an activity *within* Christianity that some may practise more than others, and some may not practise at all. Prayer is inseparable from a Christian view of reality as it is articulated in the parables of Jesus. To this extent (and much more) it is 'a gift of God and a work of his grace'. The remainder of the book will try to work out the implications of this for theory and practice.

Questions for reflection and discussion

1 'Prayer is a gift of God and a work of his grace.' Is this a helpful way of thinking about prayer? Does it challenge in any way what you have thought about the subject up to now?

2 'To practise Christianity is to practise prayer and vice versa.' Has prayer, in your experience, been thought of as an 'extra'?

If you agree that it should be absolutely central to Christian practice, in what ways can this be approached?

3 Do you feel that you have had sufficient help from your church in understanding and practising prayer, e.g. through sermons, study groups and recommended reading?

2

Prayer and the 'scientific' world-view

One of the difficulties that some people have with prayer is the suspicion that it implies a view of the world that science has shown to be improbable. The difficulty may be compounded by the suspicion that because the Bible was written so long ago, and certainly in an age that knew little about scientific causality, its statements about God and prayer cannot be taken literally; that ways must be found to translate what it says on these matters into a language and conceptuality that conform to a modern understanding of the world. There is an element of truth in these anxieties, especially if the main exposure of people to prayer is to the kind of intercessions that feature in civic and national services – what I have described as the Church of England in its pageantry mode. In these contexts a rather distant and exalted 'Almighty God' seems to function as a guarantor of a kind of status quo, with an occasional politically correct acknowledgement of the existence of the poor and needy. I hope that it has already been made clear that I do not understand prayer in this way. The present chapter will fall into two main parts: the first dealing with the biblical view of the world; the second with the scientific view of the world.

In April and June 1941 the German New Testament scholar Rudolf Bultmann delivered a lecture on 'The New Testament and Mythology' that triggered a passionate debate about how the writers of the New Testament understood the world, and how that affected modern interpretation of the New Testament. Bultmann is popularly supposed to have argued that the New

Testament writers believed in a three-storey universe, with heaven 'up there' and hell 'down there', and that because such belief was impossible in a scientific age, other ways of understanding reality, derived from modern philosophy, should provide the means for communicating the Christian message. Whether this fairly represents Bultmann's position is not the issue here. The popular version of Bultmann's lecture penetrated many areas of the Church, and it would not be surprising if there are many clergy who were taught at theological college or seminary that there was a German New Testament scholar named Bultmann, and that he was wrong![1] Whether fairly understood or not, Bultmann's lecture raised the question, important for prayer, of the nature and status of the world-views of the biblical writers.

I have argued elsewhere[2] that although people in ancient Israel had not developed anything remotely similar to modern scientific experimentation and theorizing, they had sufficient knowledge of the workings of the natural world to develop technologies that exploited natural phenomena for the benefit of human survival. They were aware of natural laws in the sense of observed regularities in the processes of nature, even if they had not formulated scientific 'laws of nature'. I argue that it is a mistake to assume that there is an unbridgeable gap between ancient Israelites and modern Western humanity when it comes to experiencing the world of nature. It is also arguable that

---

[1] See generally K. Hammann, *Rudolf Bultmann: Eine Biographie*, Tübingen: Mohr Siebeck, 2009. Details about the lecture are given on pp. 308–13. An English version of the lecture was published in H. W. Bartsch (ed.), *Kerygma and Myth*, vol. 1, London: SPCK, 1953, pp. 1–44. It is not generally appreciated that Bultmann's lecture was delivered to a society for evangelical (i.e. Protestant) theology that had been set up in 1940 to enable the Church to oppose the church politics of the Nazi regime, and that Bultmann had a distinguished record in supporting Jewish colleagues and playing a part in the so-called Confessing Church that actively opposed National Socialism.

[2] J. W. Rogerson 'The Old Testament View of Nature: Some Preliminary Questions', *Oudtestamentische Studiën* 20 (1977), pp. 67–84.

when it came to God, Israelites did not believe in a crude three-storey universe. The need for caution in this matter is shown by the following points.

The view of the world and God in the Old Testament

If an attempt is made to reconstruct the world-view that is implied in Genesis 1, it does look as though there is a kind of three-storey universe there. The earth floats on the seas, and above the earth is the firmament, a kind of dome within which sun, moon and stars move, and above which there are waters which fall upon the earth if windows in the dome are opened (see Genesis 7.11). But Genesis 1 is not the only account of the matter. In the prayer attributed to Solomon at the dedication of the temple in 1 Kings 8, the following words occur:

> But will God indeed dwell on the earth? Behold, heaven and the highest heaven cannot contain thee; how much less this house which I have built! Yet have regard to the prayer of thy servant and to his supplication, O LORD my God, hearkening to the cry and to the prayer which thy servant prays before thee this day; that thy eyes may be open night and day toward this house, the place of which thou hast said, 'My name shall be there,' that thou mayest hearken to the prayer which thy servant offers toward this place. And hearken thou to the supplication of thy servant and of thy people Israel, when they pray toward this place; yea, hear thou in heaven thy dwelling place; and when thou hearest, forgive.　　　　　(1 Kings 8.27–30)

This is a very sophisticated piece of writing. Although it addresses God in heaven towards the end of the passage, it sets out from the view that the highest heaven (Hebrew literally 'the heaven of heavens') cannot contain God; certainly, no temple built with human hands. And yet the desire of the prayer is that the temple should be a focus-point, alike for God and those who pray to him, where the human wish for forgiveness is met by divine compassion.

1 Kings 8 is not the only passage in the Old Testament that expresses a profound view of the relation of God to the created world. Psalm 139 speaks of the impossibility of escape from the divine presence:

> Whither shall I go from thy Spirit?
> Or whither shall I flee from thy presence?
> If I ascend to heaven, thou art there!
> If I make my bed in Sheol, thou art there!
> If I take the wings of the morning
> and dwell in the uttermost parts of the sea,
> even there thy hand shall lead me,
> and thy right hand shall hold me.
> If I say, 'Let only darkness cover me,
> and the light about me be night,'
> even the darkness is not dark to thee,
> the night is bright as the day;
> for darkness is as light with thee.
>
> (Psalm 139.7–12)

In Psalm 102.26–27 the heavens and the earth are likened to clothes that wear out and have to be disposed of, and have to be replaced by new ones. In contrast God is always the same, and his years have no end.

These, and other, passages show that the Old Testament writers (or at least some of them) were capable of expressing what later theology has described as the immanence and transcendence of God – the view that God is exalted above all human imagining, but that he makes himself known to people in specific ways, times and places, without this in any way compromising his exaltedness. We are a long way from 'three-storey universes' with their 'God up there'.

Science and the importance of the evidence of religious experience

There is a popular conception that in the past two hundred years or so, scientific discoveries have increasingly squeezed

God out of the world as the gaps into which he was inserted have become fewer and smaller. For many people the world can be explained completely satisfactorily in terms of scientific laws which work inexorably and leave no room for any interventions by God. If this is the truth about the world, prayer, especially intercessory prayer, is pointless. There are several strategies for dealing with this problem.

The first, well argued by Magee, is to call into question the ability of science to explain the world in terms of unalterable laws of nature. Such laws, he argues, are generalizations that cannot predict what will happen in individual cases.[3] He gives as an illustration the fact that actuaries who work for life insurance firms can forecast the life expectancy for groups of people, but not the life expectancy of individuals. Similarly, the laws of physics can predict the path of particles in a general way, but not in any particular way. Scientific laws do not, therefore, give a complete and exhaustive account of the world, and do not exclude the possibility of the action of God in it. While these points are well made, they run the danger of being sophisticated versions of the 'God of the gaps' argument. They invite the rejoinder that a time may come when it is indeed possible to forecast accurately the life expectancy of an individual, and that similar advances in physics will be able to predict the exact path of individual particles, whose present behaviour is described as random. There are two less problematic approaches.

The first is to question whether, in drawing conclusions about the nature of reality, these conclusions should be based solely upon the findings of the natural sciences. It can be argued that a wider spectrum of evidence should be taken into account, and that this evidence should include traditions about religious experience. Such traditions cannot be accepted uncritically, of course; but when the undergrowth of superstition has been

---

[3] J. B. Magee, *Reality and Prayer*, London: Hodder and Stoughton, 1958, pp. 11–19.

cleared away, sufficient remains to put the onus of proof upon those who disregard the evidence of human religious experience to justify why they do so. One of the pieces of evidence that I would emphasize is the astonishing fact that a tiny and culturally backward nation variously called Israel and Judah survived the vicissitudes of history, when the mighty and culturally more advanced cultures of Egypt, Assyria and Babylon vanished, before they were rediscovered from the nineteenth century onwards by the spades of the archaeologists. Not only did Israel/Judah survive, but it bequeathed to posterity a collection of writings whose power to challenge and inspire readers continues unabated. The persistence of Israel/Judah is not an isolated phenomenon. In a multi-faith age it is difficult not to be aware of the witness to religious experience of the religions of the East. Just as the cosmology implied in the opening chapter of Genesis cannot be considered as the last and only word about the ancient Israelite understanding of reality, so a purely scientific account of the world cannot be taken to be the only and final authority on the nature of reality.

God is not a part of our universe; he transcends it

The second approach deals with the notion of God, and how that affects our view of the world and of prayer. Particularly helpful in this regard is D. Z. Phillips's *The Concept of Prayer*.[4] Phillips argues, on the basis of a statement of Wittgenstein, that it is the task of philosophy to describe how language is actually used.[5] He accuses philosophers of religion of ignoring

---

[4] D. Z. Phillips, *The Concept of Prayer*, Oxford: Blackwell, 1981.

[5] Phillips, *Concept of Prayer*, p. 1. Wittgenstein is quoted from his *Philosophical Investigations* (trans. G. E. M. Anscombe), Oxford: Blackwell, 1953, I §124. 'Philosophy may in no way interfere with the actual use of language; it can in the end only describe it.' German: 'Die Philosophie darf den tatsächlichen Gebrauch der Sprache in keiner Weise antasten, sie kann ihn an Ende also nur beschreiben.' See Wittgenstein, *Philosophische Untersuchungen, Kritisch-genetische Edition* (ed. J. Schulte et al.), Darmstadt: Wissenschaftliche Buchgesellschaft, 2001, pp. 641, 815.

this statement, so that, instead of trying to understand and describe what is going on when people pray to God and worship (what Phillips calls the grammar of religious language), they question whether such language has any meaning. In doing this they assume that God is some kind of object within the natural world whose existence and attributes can be examined by rational thought. As Phillips puts it,

> What surprises me is that so many Christian philosophers seem to be talking about a natural, as opposed to supernatural, God; a God who is an existent among existents, and an agent among agents. What can one say to philosophers who insist on talking in this way? One can ask them to look again at the way people worship, and at what the Saints have written about their Faith . . . one must not be afraid to admit that one's arguments about religion may reach a stage where all one can say to one's opponent is, 'Well, if you can't see it, that's that!'[6]

Phillips maintains that if sense is to be made of the language used in faith and worship, then what is needed is an eternal and transcendent God, whose existence (if this is an appropriate term) is necessary and unlimited. This is another way of making the point that if we are to try to understand reality, we must take into account the evidence of religious experience and language.[7]

Phillips's argument is reassuring in the context of the present chapter, but it has serious implications that will have to be kept in view throughout this book. The fact is that some of the language of Christian prayer and worship does convey the

---

[6] Phillips, *Concept of Prayer*, p. 83.

[7] What has been called Phillips's contemplative philosophy of religion is the subject of I. U. Dalferth and H. von Sass (eds.), *The Contemplative Spirit: D. Z. Phillips on Religion and the Limits of Philosophy* (Religion in Philosophy and Theology 49), Tübingen: Mohr Siebeck, 2010. See also H. von Saas, *Sprachspiele des Glaubens: Eine Studie zur kontemplativen Religionsphilosophie von Dewi Z. Phillips mit ständiger Rücksicht auf Ludwig Wittgenstein* (Religion in Philosophy and Theology 47), Tübingen: Mohr Siebeck, 2010.

impression, and perhaps expresses the belief, that God is, if not an object within the natural world, at any rate an object that exists primarily to satisfy the needs of the human race. God is appealed to as a last resort in cases of illness where all medical options have been exhausted; he is prayed to by opposing sides in war to grant them victory. The sickening question put by journalist interviewers to believers who have just experienced a personal tragedy, 'How has this affected your faith in God?', implies that belief involves a kind of calculus according to which God is rated and believed in, in proportion to the benefits that believers suppose they derive from him. Later in this book I shall argue that it is not necessarily wrong to pray to God when we, and others known to us, face serious illness or personal difficulties. For the moment, however, I want to explore a little further the implications that God is the eternal, transcendent, God, not an object within the world.

Phillips has some useful comments here in connection with the book of Job in the Old Testament. He points out that if one has a natural God who is a part of the world, then one's view of the usefulness or goodness of this God will depend on one's fortunes in life.[8] On this criterion, Job, who loses his possessions and his family, ought to have no reason for continuing to believe in God. Yet Job does not fit this pattern, and gives a vivid example of what it means to worship a God who transcends this world as opposed to a God who is part of it. As Phillips says,

> If one attributes goodness to God by an inference from the events of one's life, it is difficult to see how Job could have avoided saying that God is evil ... But we do not find Job doing this.[9]

Of course, in the poetic part of Job (chapters 3–42), Job does seek for answers and has to defend himself against his friends,

---

[8] Phillips, *Concept of Prayer*, p. 98.
[9] Phillips, *Concept of Prayer*, p. 98.

who accuse him of having committed a great wrong to have deserved such misfortune. But his faith in God does not waver. Looking at the Old Testament as a whole, it is possible to say that it is, among other things, the story of the discovery in ancient Israel of the fact that God is the supernatural and universal Lord. He is not the kind of God that the nation wants – one to win its battles and ensure its material prosperity, regardless of its attitude to morality and social justice.

The purpose of this chapter has been to deal with the objection that prayer is pointless because science leaves no room for the God to whom prayer is made. The book will next address various aspects of the practice of prayer.

Questions for reflection and discussion

1 Do you find that living in an age in which the physical sciences are thought to explain everything makes belief in God and prayer difficult? What steps might the churches take to counter this impression?

2 If the experiences of religious people are part of the evidence that we should use to try to understand the world, how might we distinguish between 'helpful' and 'unhelpful' claims about religious experience?

3 Do we too often think of God as an object *within* the world and not as transcending it? How could thinking about God's transcendence help us in times of personal difficulty?

3

Asking God for things

————————

The type of prayer practised by most people is that of asking God for things. In the jargon of the Church it is called intercession, or petitionary prayer. It is the type of prayer most misunderstood, most abused, and most likely to lead to the loss of people's faith (in the sense of their intellectual belief in God). I hope that the previous chapter will have dealt satisfactorily with the argument that there is no point in asking God for things, because we live in a 'closed' universe governed by scientific 'laws' that leave no room for action or intervention by supernatural agencies.

There are at least four points that can be made against petitionary prayer: that it is self-centred, superstitious, unfair, and ineffective. There is truth in all these charges. A consideration of the charges, and of their strengths and weaknesses, will enable some positive points to be made.

Self-centredness

Prayers are obviously self-centred if they reduce God to a Father-Christmas-like figure, who only functions in a person's life in times of crisis, but who is conveniently ignored for the rest of the time. But it also has to be acknowledged that people who would claim to be sincere Christians and who attend church regularly will sometimes, perhaps often, find themselves asking God for things that affect their own lives or the lives of family and friends. The most obvious, and probably the most common, instances would be in the case of illness. It will be argued here that the right course of action is not to stop praying for oneself or for others, but to learn something of the grammar of such prayers, from the Bible and from Christian tradition.

The Bible is very sophisticated when it comes to the grammar of asking God for things. In the story of Solomon in 1 Kings 3, God appears to Solomon in a dream and invites him to request something. Solomon asks for 'an understanding mind to govern thy people, that I may discern between good and evil' (1 Kings 3.9). God is pleased that Solomon has not asked for long life for himself, or riches, or victory over his enemies, but that he has asked for discernment so that he can rule wisely. It is sad that the narrative about Solomon later accuses him of turning away from God (1 Kings 11.1–8); but this does not prevent the story in chapter 3 from distinguishing prayers about oneself that are aimed purely at one's own advantage (such as a request for long life, or riches, or victory) and prayers that concern how the person doing the praying relates to others.

Another class of petitionary prayer concerns the desire of individuals to be or become more faithful to God. The closing words of Psalm 139, which follow a request to God to destroy the wicked, read,

> Try me O God, and seek the ground of my heart: prove
> me, and examine my thoughts.
> Look well if there be any way of wickedness in me: and
> lead me in the way everlasting.
> (Psalm 139.23–24, Book of Common Prayer)

Coming as they do after expressing sentiments that are often considered to be unsuitable for use in public worship, they suggest that the Psalmist is well aware of the shortcomings of his attitude towards his (and God's) enemies, and is willing to have his thoughts scrutinized and corrected by God. A prayer to which, surely, no exception could be made, comes in Psalm 51.10.

> Make me a clean heart, O God: and renew a right spirit
> within me.   (Book of Common Prayer)

In the parable of the Pharisee and the Publican two types of prayer are distinguished. That of the Pharisee is a prayer of thanks to God that he is not like extortioners, adulterers and the like. It is important that we should not doubt his sincerity or his genuine gratitude. Yet the prayer that receives praise from Jesus is that of the publican: 'God, be merciful to me a sinner!' (Luke 18.13).

Many more examples of different types of petitionary prayer can be found in the Bible. What of Christian tradition? The collects of the Book of Common Prayer draw upon deep resources of the worship of the Church over many centuries. Here are some quotations chosen at random:

> Graft in our hearts the love of thy name, increase in us true religion, nourish us with all goodness, and of thy great mercy keep us in the same.   (Trinity VII)

> O God, forasmuch as without thee we are unable to please thee; Mercifully grant, that thy Holy Spirit may in all things direct and rule our hearts.   (Trinity XIX)

> Grant unto thy people, that they may love the thing which thou commandest, and desire that which thou dost promise.
> (Easter IV)

It may be objected that these collects are the prayers not of individuals, but of congregations. This is true, but the assumption of the collects is that the individuals that make up the congregation will own or claim the sentiments expressed in the collects as their own individual prayers.

What this brief excursion into the Bible and Christian tradition indicates is that asking God for things for oneself is not necessarily wrong. To ask for forgiveness, discernment, renewal, understanding, while centred on the self, also transcends the self and looks to an interaction with the world that will be a process of giving, much more than receiving. This still leaves open the matter of whether it is right to pray for oneself at a time of illness, or when facing an examination, or with regard to employment. These topics will be dealt with later.

Superstition

Phillips has a helpful chapter entitled 'Superstition and Petitionary Prayer',[1] and what follows is partially indebted to him. The key in distinguishing superstition from (true) petitionary prayer lies, for Phillips, in the notion of dependence. He contrasts the prayer of a diver searching a wreck, who lost his torch and could not find the way out from where he was, with that of the Psalmist in Psalm 23.4.[2] The diver prayed, 'O God get me out of this. I'll do anything you want if only you'll let me find my way out.' The Psalmist affirmed, 'Yea, though I walk through the valley of the shadow of death I will fear no evil, for thou art with me.' Phillips argues that the diver assumes two things: that God *could* intervene to save him from danger, and that God would have a reason for saving him rather than letting him die. The Psalmist, on the other hand, does not shrink from death but faces it in the confidence that he can rely upon God. In Phillips's view, the diver's attitude amounts to superstition. Another example of superstition given by Phillips is the remark of a mother whose prayer that her child might not die was not successful: 'Did I not pray hard enough?' Phillips sees this as akin to 'The spell was not powerful enough.'[3]

---

[1] D. Z. Phillips, *The Concept of Prayer*, Oxford: Blackwell, 1981, pp. 112–30.
[2] Phillips, *Concept of Prayer*, p. 117.
[3] Phillips *Concept of Prayer*, p. 118.

These observations are helpful, but they suffer from one weakness if they appear to classify those who are being superstitious with those who are generally indifferent to God, and those who are genuinely praying with those who generally take God seriously. It is not as simple as that, and there are undoubtedly examples of petitionary prayer's becoming, or bordering on, superstition among people who would be offended to be told that they were generally indifferent to God. Here are some examples.

The first is the belief in some Christian circles that if the number of people praying for a certain issue can be multiplied, then the outcome is more likely to be favourable (i.e. the people praying get the result that *they* want). The implication seems to be that God is impressed or overwhelmed by numbers; that he will grant a request if two hundred people pray about it, but not if only two do. This is surely not much different from Phillips's 'The spell was not powerful enough.' Another technique that one might encounter is that in which a person praying holds God to account. God is reminded that he has power, and that he has made promises to answer prayers. The person praying presses claims upon God, demands that God should fulfil his promises. The name and 'for the sake of' Jesus Christ are invoked in order to add to the efficacy of the prayer. Again, this is reminiscent of 'The spell was not powerful enough.' Does this mean that Christians should not enlist the help of others in praying for a particular need? No; no harm can be done by inviting people to pray for the needs of others so long as they are aware that there is no way of knowing how God uses their prayers. The use of language to God that implies that he must be faithful to his promises is not something to which I respond positively, in spite of the fact that such sentiments appear to be expressed in some of the psalms (e.g. Psalms 74 and 79).

Bearing in mind the examples from Phillips, and those that I have given from Christian practice, I would say that the dividing line between superstition and 'genuine' prayer is not always easy to draw, and that Christians are as liable as non-Christians to 'pray' superstitiously. Perhaps the decisive factor is whether, in petition, God is being used simply as a tool for the furtherance of human desires. Ideally, all petitionary prayers should end with, or at least imply, the words of Jesus in the Garden of Gethsemane: 'yet not what I will, but what thou wilt' (Mark 14.36).[4]

One objection to what has been written here may be that in the Gospels Jesus teaches the necessity of persistence in prayer. The imperatives in the words 'Ask, and it will be given you; seek, and you will find; knock, and it will be opened to you' (Matthew 7.7; Luke 11.9) are imperfect imperatives in the Greek, implying that one should keep on asking, seeking and knocking.[5] In Luke 11, these words are preceded by the parable of the Importunate Neighbour (Luke 11.5–8). A friend arrives at a person's house at midnight. The host, having no food to give him, goes to his neighbour, requesting that he lend him three loaves. The neighbour, however, is not inclined to respond. To do so will involve disturbing the whole household. But Jesus implies that even if the neighbour will not get up and give him the loaves because he has been asked to do so by a friend, he will do so if the neighbour who is making the request is persistent. He will tire of the neighbour's knocking and entreating, and agree with the request for the sake of the peace and quiet that will ensue. A similar parable occurs at Luke 18.1–8. A judge who is requested by a widow to give her vindication against an adversary eventually does so, not because of the rightness of the case, but because the widow wears him out

---

[4] See also Phillips, *Concept of Prayer*, p. 122.

[5] Jesus, of course, spoke in Aramaic, and in common with other Semitic languages, Aramaic imperatives do not distinguish between giving a command to do something once, and giving a command to do something repeatedly. A longer construction is needed to do this.

with her persistent pestering. What are we to make of these parables? One conclusion might be that petitionary prayer is, after all, more likely to succeed if it is backed by effort and numbers. It may be an inducement to make the spell as powerful as possible. This, however, would be to misunderstand the parables. Their point is not that God can be persuaded to do what we want if we are persistent in our requests. They are examples of the 'how much more' argument often found in the teaching of Jesus and, indeed, that of other Jewish teachers of the period. It occurs in the parables of the Lost Sheep and Lost Coin (Luke 15.7, 10). The point is that if reluctant neighbours and judges can be moved to action by persistence, how much more is God prepared to respond to petitions, who is not reluctant and does not need persistence. This does not mean, of course, that we shall get what we think we want. As T. W. Manson remarked, commenting on the parable of the Importunate Neighbour, 'it may be that it is only by telling God frankly what we want that we can learn what we truly need'.[6]

Unfairness

If there is any point in praying to God that he will help other people, is not this unfair? Let us suppose that Mrs A, who is seriously ill, has friends at her local church who are praying for her. At the same time, Mrs Y, who is seriously ill with the same medical condition as Mrs A, has no one to pray for her. Does this mean that whereas God might do something for Mrs A, because she is supported in prayer, he is unlikely to do anything for Mrs Y, because she is not? And if he does favour

---

[6] T. W. Manson, in H. D. A. Major, T. W. Manson and C. J. Wright, *The Mission and Message of Jesus: An Exposition of the Gospels in the Light of Modern Research*, London: Ivor Nicholson and Watson, 1937, p. 559.

Mrs Y, does that not mean that the prayers offered on behalf of Mrs A were a waste of time?

Although what follows is not a particularly satisfactory answer to this question, it is at least realistic. The fact is that we live in a very unfair world. Returning to Mrs A and Mrs Y, it may well be that Mrs A is not only lucky enough to have people to pray for her; she may be supported by a loving family whose members live sufficiently close to her to be able to visit and care for her at all hours of the night and the day. Mrs Y's family may be scattered around the country, or even the world, so that none of its members are able to do more than make occasional visits. Examples of such apparent unfairness can easily be multiplied. They can be extended to take in the point that even to be born in a poor part of the Western world may be more fortunate than being born in a country that lacks clean drinking water and basic medicines. Even the communication of the Christian gospel is subject to the same aspects of unfairness. Some people are born into believing families; many are not. Some benefit from inspiring clergy or teachers or friends; others do not. There is nothing that can be done on the grand scale to alter these unfairnesses overnight. Individuals who are challenged by them will do what they can in the situations in which they find themselves. Insofar as these unfairnesses affect praying for other people, there may be two strategies that can be adopted. The first is to be aware of the unfairnesses, and to include them in one's prayers. In praying for a sick person, one might also include a petition for those who have no one to pray for them. The other strategy is to use, as well as prayers for individuals, prayers of a general nature, of which there are many examples.

All this, of course, begs another question. Does God need our prayers in order to carry out his work? If he does, then surely he is party to the unfairnesses. If he does not need our prayers, why do we go on offering them?

A. D. Belden wrote:

Pure and fervent petition enlarges God's opportunity of working in human affairs. . . . We have to pray for the same reason that we have to think and work, because only so can the good and wise God find full opportunity of doing what his goodness and wisdom desire.[7]

I do not agree with all of this. I do not agree, for example, that God can only do what he wants to do if we make it possible. There are two positive things about Belden's statement, however. The first is that God's dealings with the world are in some way helped by our actions. A telephone call that we make, a letter that we write, a visit that we arrange, a gift of money that we send – these may all be ways in which God reaches out through us to other people. Also, and this is an important point to which I shall return, it may be God who is prompting us to do these things. The second point is that prayer for others may be similar to activities such as telephoning, letter-writing, visiting or sending money, in that they are a kind of cooperation with God, not a set of requests sent to an indifferent deity.

Ineffectiveness

Here we touch on the most problematic aspect of petitionary prayer – the fact that many prayers appear to go unanswered, that is to say, that people do not get the results that they wish for, having prayed about a particular matter. There are, of course, various anodyne ways of explaining this, including the stock answer that God always answers prayers in one of three ways – yes, no, or wait. This has always smacked to me of the 'heads I win – tails you lose' type of argument, an argument that is too slick and clever to be convincing.

It seems to me to be an inescapable fact that many people would claim that in particular instances their prayers appear

---

[7] A. D. Belden, *The Practice of Prayer*, London: Rockliff, 1954, pp. 30, 34.

to have been answered. They may all have been mistaken, of course; but the conviction and sincerity with which such claims can be made make me want to take them seriously. If, as argued above (p. 16), part of the way in which we understand the world is based upon the evidence of religious experience, then the conviction of believers that prayers have been answered must be taken into account. It will also, hopefully, be true that those who are convinced that prayers have been answered will also agree that in other, or perhaps many, cases, they have not been answered (i.e. the outcome has not been what they desired). The problem is particularly obvious where prayers are offered for people whose medical condition has brought them close to death. Many people would say that they know cases in which they sincerely believed that the persons prayed for had staged remarkable recoveries. In other cases, where the prayer was offered just as sincerely, the person being prayed for did not recover. What are we to make of this? The answer that we give may depend on where we are coming from. Those whose prayer is close to superstition may be so impressed by the apparent randomness of the process, that they may conclude that prayer is a waste of time and that people who believe that their prayers have been 'answered' are mistaken. Those for whom God is more than a means of enhancing their own happiness may see things differently. The 'answers' that they believe that they have received will not be compromised by apparent failures in prayer. These 'answers' will help to assure them that their commitment to God is not in vain.

Another factor that needs to be introduced at this point is that of guidance. Many Christians, looking back over their lives, will feel that in some respects they have been guided. The 'guidance' may take many forms: chance encounters that have proved to be life-changing or that were turning-points in life; employment opportunities presenting themselves at exactly the right time; or the reading of a particular book or the hearing of a particular sermon that came at just the right time to affect thinking or doing. The feeling that in these 'coincidences' the working of God could be glimpsed may, of course, be a delusion, a false interpretation of what could be explained without the need for God. Yet it is experiences such as these that have moved people from thinking of God merely as an idea to making them convinced that God is an active force in the world. It is a conviction that has caused some to become missionaries or in some other way to follow a career path that they may never previously have contemplated or even thought possible. It is a conviction that has sustained them at times when the life of faith seemed pointless or perverse. The importance of guidance for the present discussion is that it helps those who have caught glimpses of having lived a guided life to embrace that connectedness with God that makes the difference between petitionary prayer being prayer, and being superstition. This is in spite of the fact that they, too, will sometimes pray in a way that is, or borders on, superstition. The important thing is that a sense of being guided, even if this is apparent only to hindsight, will or should affect the way in which petitionary prayer is understood. It will not be supplication to a distant deity with whom otherwise one has no connection. It will be part of a spectrum of connections that will include worship, service, study and action.

God as the initiator of petitionary prayer

It is now time to introduce and consider a paradox. In the first chapter John Magee was quoted as saying that 'prayer is a gift of God and a work of his grace'. Mother Mary Clare SLG has written, 'The first lesson we have to learn about prayer . . . is that it is God's activity in us and not a self-activated process of our own.'[8] If this seems odd, it can be paralleled by statements

---

[8] Mother Mary Clare SLG, *Learning to Pray*, Oxford: SLG Press, 2nd ed. 2006, p. 5.

in the Bible and in traditional prayers. Paul writes in Romans
8.26–7,

> the Spirit helps us in our weakness; for we do not know how to
> pray as we ought, but the Spirit himself intercedes for us with
> sighs too deep for words. And he who searches the hearts of
> men knows what is the mind of the Spirit, because the Spirit
> intercedes for the saints according to the will of God.

The collect for Trinity III includes the words 'grant that we,
to whom thou hast given an hearty desire to pray . . .'.[9] These
sentiments, if true, turn on its head the usual way in which we
think about petitionary prayer. Our normal view is that we
are taking the initiative in bringing matters to God's attention,
about which we hope he will do something. But if the initiative
comes from God, the whole matter appears in a different light.
He is moving us to pray for things about which he is concerned,
not vice versa.

This idea, if true, is so important that it must be subjected
to the same critical questioning as the view that it is we
who take the initiative in approaching God. If God takes the
initiative, why are so many of our prayers apparently unanswered? If God is moving us to pray for someone who is
critically ill, this implies that God desires that person's
recovery. What if he or she does not recover? What about
our prayers for ourselves, that we may pass an examination,
or be successful in a job interview, or that the person we
have just fallen in love with may feel the same about us?
There is no satisfactory answer to these questions; but it is
important that we should ask them. What follows now does
not pretend to give any satisfactory answers, but rather to
present a perspective in which we may see the questions
differently.

---

[9] See also Mother Mary Clare, *Learning*, p. 12, 'The Holy Spirit is the initiator of all
prayer, which is a gift from God.'

That God takes the initiative in human affairs is a presupposition of the Bible from the first page to the last. The creation is God's initiative, as is the call of Abram (Genesis 12), the commissioning of Moses (Exodus 3), the calling of the prophets (Amos 7.15; Jeremiah 1.5; Ezekiel 2.3), the birth of Jesus (Luke 1.30–31), the calling of the first disciples (Mark 1.16–20) and the conversion of Paul (1 Corinthians 15.8–10). Many Christians, looking back on their lives, may feel that they can endorse the words in John 15.16, 'you did not choose me, but I chose you'. What this amounts to is that Christians are, or should be, enlisted in the mission of God to fulfil the purpose of the creation, to establish a realm of peace, harmony and justice that will include the non-human part of the created order (Psalm 96.10–13; Isaiah 65.17–25). The obstacles to the achieving of this purpose are formidable, deriving as they do from the freedom that God has given to his creatures to choose or reject him. The obstacles are not just the sum of the ignorance of individuals or their opposition to God. God's freedom has allowed a space for evil to fashion its own realm, a realm that draws its strength from the failure of humans to be truly human, and which creates structures that allow oppression and injustice to take root in human societies. The main weapon that God deploys in this struggle is that of self-giving, suffering love, something that is exemplified in the ministry and passion of Jesus, and is very occasionally visible in the work of the Church and the lives of Christians.

As applied to petitionary prayer, this approach enables the quotation from Belden (see above, p. 29) to be reformulated as follows:

Pure and fervent petition enlarges God's opportunity of working in human affairs. We have to pray for the same reason that we have to think, and study, and plan, and work, because this is how God uses us to further his purposes in the world, while at the same time he works in ways that we can neither know nor understand.

It puts our prayers for ourselves and others into a different perspective. It is not wrong, in my view, to pray about our careers or our love life, or the health and well-being of others; but we need to ask why we are praying about these things. Is it because a favourable answer will enable us to do God's will more effectively? Will it further his kingdom and purposes? Are our prayers for the recovery from illness of family and friends at least partly motivated by compassion, by the conviction that illness and the death of someone well short of the prime of life are not part of the ideal will of God?[10] Are such prayers a way of saying 'thy kingdom come'? If so, they are justified, so long as we are also aware that the ideal will of God can be frustrated by human wickedness and structural evil. If so, an 'unanswered' prayer should not be regarded as a failure but should move us to a deeper appreciation of the suffering of God as glimpsed in the passion of Jesus. It should move us to deeper commitment. Petitionary prayer can be thought of as a ministry to which God calls us.

A model for intercession based upon Mark 2.1–12

The following interpretation of Mark 2.1–12 apparently derives from Hedley Hodkin (1902–95), although I did not hear it from him directly.[11] The passage tells of how four men brought a paralytic man to Jesus in Capernaum. Because they could not

---

[10] The ideal will of God is what God would want in a world that was without evil and suffering and resistance to his laws. This world does not exist within time and space.

[11] Hedley Hodkin was born in Sheffield, ordained as a Methodist minister, and became an Anglican, serving as vicar of Holy Trinity, Millhouses, Sheffield, and canon residentiary of Manchester Cathedral, where I came into contact with him while I was a student.

get into the house where Jesus was, they climbed onto the roof, made an opening, and let down the bed on which the paralytic was lying, in front of Jesus. Jesus, seeing their faith, told the paralytic that his sins were forgiven. This caused offence to some of those present, on the ground that only God could forgive sins. Jesus asked them whether it was easier to say that a person's sins were forgiven, or to say, 'arise, and take up thy bed, and go thy way' (AV). To demonstrate that 'the Son of man has authority on earth to forgive sins', Jesus commanded the man to take up his bed and walk, which he did, to the astonishment of those present.

Hedley Hodkin's use of the passage concentrated upon the first part – the fact that four men who believed that Jesus could help their friend translated that belief into action that refused to be daunted by practical difficulties such as transporting the man, and bringing him to the attention of Jesus, when there was no access to him because of the crowds surrounding him. Jesus responded to their faith, to their determination to bring the paralysed man to him. His reply, however, was surprising. It was obvious what was wrong with the man physically; yet Jesus said that his sins were forgiven.

Hodkin made the following points. If we bring the needs of others to Jesus in prayer, he responds to our faith in his ability to help. The response of Jesus, however, may not be what we expect. We think that we know what needs to be done. Jesus knows better. We should be prepared, therefore, to bring the needs of others to Jesus, but to withdraw, as it were, before he says anything in reply to the person in need. That is not our business. Our task is complete once we have brought the person to Jesus.

I have found this to be a helpful way of thinking about intercession. It emphasizes the importance of the initiative that we take, even if, as suggested earlier, we believe that God is urging us to take the initiative. I can use the incident to engage my imagination in intercession. I can picture Jesus sitting in the house surrounded by the crowd listening to his teaching, and I can imagine interrupting him by placing the person for whom I am praying in his presence. At this point I withdraw. I can do no more. I am content to leave that person in the presence of the one who knows best what is needed, and who knows what can be achieved in a world that is marred by much that is far from the ideal will of God.

Questions for reflection and discussion

1 Describe or recall occasions on which you are convinced that your prayers have been answered. Can you think of any reason why they seem to have been answered?

2 How can we avoid making God into a tool for doing what we want to happen?

3 Do you find it helpful to think of God taking the initiative in moving us to ask for things?

4

Confession

It is not often that a scholar publishes a book that completely changes how people think about a subject, but this was what the German theologian Rudolf Otto achieved in 1917 with the appearance of his *The Idea of the Holy*.[1] Otto argued that the roots of the concept of holiness lay in experiences in which people became aware of something terrifying, or awesomely overwhelming or beautiful, as a result of which they felt insignificant and powerless in the presence of something that could not be explained rationally. Although Otto did not regard this as a specifically religious experience, in that it could happen in non-religious settings such as the world of nature, he also identified it within religious observance. Otto used phrases such as 'the Wholly Other', 'the numinous' and 'mysterium tremendum' to describe that which was encountered in such experiences, and these phrases, as well as 'the sacred', quickly found their way into the vocabulary of the study of religions. Because Otto, while being a Christian theologian, did not identify 'the Wholly Other' specifically with God, his work has been influential in the comparative study of religions.

---

[1] R. Otto, *Das Heilige: Über das Irrationale in der Idee des Göttlichen und sein Verhältnis zum Rationalen*, Munich: C. H. Beck, 1917. Reference is made to the 25th ed. 1936. ET *The Idea of the Holy: An Inquiry into the Non-rational Factor in the Idea of the Divine and its Relation to the Rational*, Harmondsworth: Penguin, 1959.

The importance of Otto for the present chapter is that he interpreted several passages in the Bible in terms of an encounter with 'the Wholly Other', drawing attention to the reaction of the humans involved, and their confession of feeling utterly powerless and insignificant in the presence of what they had encountered. The most important reference is to Isaiah 6.1–8.[2] The prophet has a vision in which he sees the exalted God of Israel and hears the voices of the angelic seraphim chanting 'Holy, Holy, Holy'. Apparently, Otto had himself been deeply moved by hearing these words chanted in a Sephardic synagogue in Morocco.[3] The reaction of the prophet is that he cries out in anguish:

> Woe is me! For I am lost; for I am a man of unclean lips, and I dwell in the midst of a people of unclean lips; for my eyes have seen the King, the LORD of hosts!

The Hebrew verb *nidmeyti*, rendered here as 'lost', properly means 'ruined' or 'destroyed', and Hans Wildberger, in his commentary on Isaiah, also drawing attention to the word 'woe', remarks that the language used here is that of a person who feels that his very existence is threatened, and that a lament over his death is already being performed.[4] This fits well with Otto's description of the feeling of utter insignificance in the presence of 'the Wholly Other'.

Another passage to which Otto refers is the call of Peter in Luke 5.1–8. Jesus asks Peter to let him use his boat as a place from which to address the crowds by the shore of the Sea of Galilee. Having finished his teaching, Jesus tells Peter to sail to a deep part of the lake and to cast his nets. This Peter does,

[2] Otto, *Idea of the Holy*, German p. 82, English, p. 78.
[3] See C. Crowder, 'Otto's *The Idea of the Holy* revisited' in S. C. Barton (ed.), *Holiness Past and Present*, London: T. & T. Clark, 2003, pp. 45–6.
[4] H. Wildberger, *Jesaja 1–12* (Biblischer Kommentar Altes Testament), Neukirchen-Vluyn: Neukirchener Verlag, 1972, p. 251.

in spite of having fished all night without catching anything. When an enormous shoal of fish is caught, Peter is astonished. He senses that he is in the presence of someone remarkable and cries out, 'Depart from me, for I am a sinful man, O Lord' (Luke 5.8).

The importance of these passages for the present chapter is that they set the standard, in my view, for that aspect of prayer called confession. Whether or not we have ever had an encounter with the sacred that tallies with Otto's descriptions, we may well have had lesser moments of uplift, especially in worship. We may have been lifted up away from ourselves, so to speak, and have glimpsed beauties and possibilities that have deeply moved us.

When I say that such experiences should set the standard for confession, what I have in mind is this. In our church services we are regularly required to use forms of confession in which we say, among other things, that we are sorry for our sins, and ask God to forgive us. It may be difficult on some, or most, occasions to feel truly sorry; and there is the added difficulty that since childhood we have known and used the word 'sorry' as a kind of truce word – a word that we knew would assuage the anger of parents or teachers even when (as in most cases) we did not feel any remorse for what we had done and had no intention of putting things right even if we could. This tends to make the confession part of our services a meaningless exercise, and one not helped by the anodyne sentiments that masquerade as forms of confession.

It is easy to be critical of the forms of confession found in the Book of Common Prayer, and my main complaint would be that they concentrate entirely on individual failings and make no mention of the corporate and structural aspects of wickedness. That having been said, it is not possible to doubt their serious diagnosis of the individual human condition in the presence of God.

> We have erred, and strayed from thy ways like lost sheep. We have followed too much the devices and desires of our own hearts. We have offended against thy holy laws. We have left undone those things that we ought to have done; And we have done those things that we ought not to have done; And there is no health in us. (from the General Confession)

If we cannot say these words sincerely, perhaps we have to ask how we conceive of ourselves in relation to God. I am not suggesting that we should indulge in an orgy of pity or self-denigration; rather, that these words (or better ones if we can find them) should help us to acknowledge how insignificant we are compared with the incomparable and unimaginable greatness of God. It is too easy for the grace of God to become cheap, for God's forgiveness to be something that we take for granted; for it to be automatically presumed because a priest has pronounced an absolution. In worship we need to be helped to steer a middle course between the kind of ceremonial that becomes an end in itself and obscures God because of an obsession with getting ceremonial details 'right', and the kind of informality that reduces God to trivial levels. This is a challenging task for those who arrange and conduct worship. Personally, I dislike hymns that are not really addressed to God but are reminders to the congregation of the many injustices in the world. These injustices are obviously matters of considerable importance in any understanding of Christianity and should have a place in prayer, preaching and action. Whether they should feature in hymns is another matter.

What this chapter is tending to say is that confession is not so much a matter of saying 'sorry'. It is more to do with achieving a sense of the awesomeness of God. To the extent that this is achieved, words become unnecessary. The masks that we wear are torn off, and the roles that we play become transparent to us, even if not to others. (They may, of course, be plainly visible to others!) These moments of great honesty and great weakness are prime opportunities for the Spirit of God to enter parts of our lives that have previously been inaccessible. If feelings of dissatisfaction are experienced, these can be welcomed as signs of the presence of the Spirit of God.

There are practical steps that can be taken in the quest for a sense of the awesomeness of God. One is a proper appreciation of the Lord's Prayer. The fact that it is recited so frequently makes it a prime candidate for helping us to lose touch with the awesome majesty of God. There is an urgent need for serious preaching and teaching about its meaning and significance. Another German theologian, Ernst Lohmeyer, wrote of the Lord's Prayer as presented in Matthew 6.9–13 that it is

> the basic prayer for the eschatological community of the disciples, not a prayer for individuals, but for the community, not for the necessities of human life but for the requirements of the life of a disciple, life in this eschatological time, which will presently emerge from its hiddenness into the eternal light of the eschatological day of God.[5]

Lohmeyer wrote these words during the Second World War, not long before he was murdered by the Soviet authorities in September 1946 in their occupation zone of Germany, on false charges of crimes against the Soviet people. Although Lohmeyer generally emphasized the eschatological dimension of the teaching of Jesus (that is, he saw the ministry of Jesus as a time of crisis in which the kingdom of God was breaking into the world), his work on the Lord's Prayer was no doubt affected by the times of crisis in which he wrote.[6] Nonetheless,

---

[5] E. Lohmeyer, *The Lord's Prayer*, London: Collins, 1965, p. 21. I have been unable to obtain the German original, *Das Vater-Unser*, Göttingen: Vandenhoeck & Ruprecht, 1952.

[6] More about Lohmeyer's life can be found in A. Köhn, *Der Neutestamentler Ernst Lohmeyer: Studien zu Biographie und Theologie* (Wissenschaftliche Untersuchungen zum Neuen Testament 2. Reihe 180), Tübingen: Mohr Siebeck, 2004; J. R. Edwards, 'Lohmeyer, Ernst (1890–1946)' in D. K. McKim (ed.), *Dictionary of Major Biblical Interpreters*, Nottingham: Inter-Varsity Press, 2007, pp. 671–5.

his insights remain exciting and demanding. He saw the Lord's Prayer as something given to the first disciples to equip them for service in the time of crisis in which they found themselves. Its purpose was not to enable them to pray for the necessities of life in a world that was existing serenely and peacefully. It was a prayer full of urgency. The request for God's name to be hallowed (that is, made holy) was not a request that people should treat God's name with reverence. It was a request that God should act to make his justice and majesty visible in the world. In the context of the present chapter it can be interpreted as a request that the world should become aware of God's awesome presence, a presence that would strip its inhabitants bare of all pretensions, and leave them powerless, and spiritually and morally naked. Although this chapter is not the place for a detailed exposition of the Lord's Prayer,[7] others of its clauses bear the same sense of urgency. 'Give us this day our daily bread' more accurately means 'give us tomorrow's bread today', 'tomorrow's bread' being the bread served at the heavenly banquet of God's consummated kingdom.[8] 'Lead us not into temptation' is better rendered 'do not bring us to the time of trial'[9], the request being for strength when disciples are tested by persecution and misunderstanding in their work and witness to the coming kingdom of God.

Two points follow from the attempt to take seriously the awesome nature of the God who calls us to his service. The first, worship, has already been mentioned, and how it needs to convey the sense of God's greatness and majesty, whatever else it tries to do. The second is lifestyle. Lifestyle involves seeing

---

[7] This is done in Chapter 6.

[8] See U. Luz, *Das Evangelium nach Matthäus* (Evangelisch-Katholischer Kommentar zum Neuen Testament I/1), Zürich: Benzinger Verlag; Neukirchen-Vluyn: Neukirchener Verlag, 1985, pp. 345–7.

[9] See E. Lohse, *Vater Unser: Das Gebet der Christen*, Darmstadt: Wissenschaftliche Buchgesellschaft, 2nd ed. 2010, pp. 76–83.

things from a transcendent and eschatological perspective. Just as familiar landscapes can look quite different when viewed from above, as for example by aerial or satellite photographs, so familiar problems of daily life can be transformed when viewed from the perspective of God's eternity. Things that seem important become trivial; problems that appear to be mountainous are seen to be no more than gentle slopes.

This chapter may appear to have strayed a long way from the subject of confession. This has been deliberate. The aim of the chapter has been to rescue the subject of confession from being an irksome item in public worship in which we are not sure whether we have anything to confess anyway, except perhaps things about which we can do little directly, such as world poverty. The intention has been to connect confession with becoming aware of the awesome majesty of God, and our utter insignificance in his presence.

Questions for reflection and discussion

1 What are the good things about the form(s) of confession used in the services in your church? What are the bad things? What items would an ideal form of confession include?

2 Should the word 'sorry' be banned from forms of confession used in church services?

3 Should church services always include a form of confession?

5

Affirmation, meditation, mysticism and prayers for the dead

———•◆•———

Affirmation

I can still remember the help that I got from reading a series of sermons by Leslie Weatherhead on the Twenty-Third Psalm.[1] At the time I was completing my national service at the Royal Air Force station, Habbaniyah, Iraq. The Christian fellowship that I attended on Wednesday evenings, when my shift work allowed me to do so, was dominated by members of the Open Brethren and other nonconformists. They had a very distinctive way of praying and spent much time asking God to be with them and to bless them. Weatherhead's words in his opening chapter therefore struck me forcibly:

> this Psalm . . . strikes a positive note. It is not beseeching God to be something or to do something. It is stating positively that He *is* and *does* all that is required by man. The writer does not say 'Oh Lord, be my Shepherd. Make me to lie down in green pastures: lead me beside the still waters.' He is asserting these very things and glorying in them.[2]

Later in the book, Weatherhead said similar things about the clause 'Yea, though I walk through the valley of the shadow of death, I will fear no evil; for Thou art with me.'

---

[1] L. D. Weatherhead, *A Shepherd Remembers: A Devotional Study of the Twenty-Third Psalm*, London: Hodder and Stoughton, 1937.

[2] Weatherhead, *A Shepherd Remembers*, p. 25.

44

The Psalmist . . . does not ask that he may be taken round another way and so escape the valley of gloom . . . He does not even ask that he may not be afraid. He *affirms*, that he will not be afraid, because – and then he writes down one of the greatest truths in the world – *God will be there, too* . . . The evil may have to be faced. It cannot always be evaded. But, 'I will *fear* no evil. *For Thou art with me.*'[3]

He went on to point out the change of person from the third to the second person. 'He is not writing *about* a person now. He is *talking* to a person: *Thou* art with me.'[4]

Many years later Weatherhead published a book in which he suggested that praying could be imagined as passing successively through seven different rooms in a house, and he equipped each room with appropriate furniture in the form of quotations from the Bible, hymns, prayers and poems, for each of 30 days.[5] The first room was one in which the presence of God was *affirmed*. Here are just a few of the biblical passages that he used. To Jacob: 'Behold, I am with you and will keep you wherever you go' (Genesis 28.15); to Moses: 'I will be with you' (Exodus 3.12); to Joshua: 'as I was with Moses, so I will be with you; I will not fail you or forsake you' (Joshua 1.5). The Psalmist affirms: 'Whither shall I go from thy Spirit? Or whither shall I flee from thy presence?' (Psalm 139.7). The risen Jesus says to his disciples: 'Lo, I am with you always, to the close of the age' (Matthew 28.20).

Affirmation is arguably the most important aspect of prayer. It involves trusting God to be true to his promises. If this cannot be done, what kind of God is prayed to in worship or confession? There are many biblical texts that declare God's promises that he will be with his people, to sustain and guide

---

[3] Weatherhead, *A Shepherd Remembers*, p. 125.

[4] Weatherhead, *A Shepherd Remembers*, p. 125.

[5] L. D. Weatherhead, *A Private House of Prayer*, London: Hodder and Stoughton, 1958.

them. To take them on trust, and to live as though they were true, leads to becoming ever more sure that they are, in fact, true. Of course, it is important that in affirming the presence of God we do not overlook what this involves. It involves the willingness of God, whose being is beyond anything we can imagine, and in whose presence we are at best dust and ashes, to enter into the petty details of our lives. It involves God's loving and accepting us in spite of our unworthiness, our failures and our disloyalties. It is, indeed, 'a gift of God, and a work of his grace'.

Closely allied to the practice of affirmation is the practice of God's presence, as famously described in the conversations and letters of Brother Lawrence.[6] Brother Lawrence, born Nicolas Herman (*c*.1614–91), became a Carmelite friar in Paris, having served as a soldier in the Thirty Years War, in which he was badly wounded. His work in the monastery was as a cook and repairer of shoes. Finding less help in the formal services of his order, he developed a way of realizing God's presence in all that he did. Typical of his observations is the following:

> think often on God, by day, by night, in your business, and even in your diversions. He is always near you and with you; leave Him not alone. You would think it rude to leave a friend alone, who came to visit you; why then must God be neglected?[7]

To begin to try to make a habit of this has many advantages, especially for those whose circumstances make it difficult to have a set time or times of prayer each day. Obviously, if it is possible to set aside a space and time each day for prayer, that should be done. But not everyone in the rush and business

---

[6] There are many editions of *The Practice of the Presence of God: The Best Rule of a Holy Life Being Conversations and Letters of Brother Lawrence*. The edition used here was published by Epworth Press (no date).

[7] Brother Lawrence, *Practice*, p. 52.

of today's world finds this possible; and in any case, people's temperaments vary greatly when it comes to prayer. There is no 'one size fits all' for prayer, and perhaps more people than we realize have been hindered from praying because they were taught or confronted by models of praying that were not suited to them. This may also be true, of course, of the practice of God's presence in the everyday. What helps one person does not necessarily help another!

Meditation

I take meditation to mean those occasions when we try to understand the things of God more clearly or deeply; and here, I am at a disadvantage in writing about the subject. As an academic and professional biblical scholar, I have had, and continue to have, opportunities to read and think about Christian faith that are denied to most people. It is too easy for me to take far too much for granted when teaching or preaching. What I write here may be of little or no help. There is a further difficulty. Although I use the internet for various purposes, I am not a 'natural' user in the way that young people are. I am not aware of the resources available on the internet for studying Christian doctrine, or even for praying; and I must not rule out the likelihood that the internet is already enabling people to devise and use methods of prayer that are appropriate to an electronic and communicative age. Bearing these potential weaknesses in mind, I set out the following thoughts.

People often imply to me that there are two ways of reading the Bible – academically and devotionally; and that the two ways are mutually exclusive. This has never been my experience. Obviously, the academic study of the Bible can involve highly technical matters that have no obviously immediate connection with Christian faith and practice, and I regularly read books of this technical nature. But such books are irrelevant to faith only if we choose to define 'devotion' or 'meditation' in a narrow way, for example, in terms of something that gives us a spiritual shot in the arm. In any case, it is not advisable to judge the success or otherwise of meditation by the extent to which we are uplifted by it. If we do, we can easily fall into the trap of meditating in order to get something out of it. God then becomes merely a vehicle for our own satisfaction. Meditation should be done for its own sake; experiences of 'uplift' are by-products, for which we can be thankful to God, but which should not be sought as the primary goal.

In view of the above, I would not want to confine meditation to a devotional-type reading of a passage from the Bible, important as that is. I would include in meditation the study of the historical backgrounds to the Old and New Testaments, the study of the history of the Church – any study, indeed, that enlarged our understanding of the historical and philosophical aspects of Christian faith. I would encourage people to enrol for evening classes in such subjects, if local churches are not providing any opportunities for study, and would encourage people to think and say that they were doing something that was devotional as well as academic. The artificial distinction between 'academic' and 'devotional' is no doubt partly responsible for the widespread ignorance of the fundamentals of Christian faith among many churchgoers, as well as the insistence on the part of some clergy that their congregations require only 'simple faith'.

Particularly in evangelical circles, great importance is laid upon the daily reading of the Bible; and various daily Bible reading schemes exist. They are also no doubt provided on the internet. Daily Bible reading is much to be encouraged, provided that it does not become a substitute for further study as described in the preceding paragraph. There is also the point that the life schedules for some people may make daily reading very difficult, or impossible, while others, with the best of intentions, may fall behind in their use of a daily Bible reading scheme, and then give up altogether, crushed by the regime required. There are other possibilities. There are many devotional biblical commentaries that allow users to go at their own speed, and do not impose a dated, daily scheme. There are collections of sermons and other books about Christian faith and practice that can justifiably be used under the heading of meditation.

The word 'contemplation' is also found in books on prayer and the Christian life. I am not sure that I know whether there is a difference between meditation and contemplation, and accordingly will say nothing further about the subject here.

Mysticism

This section will concern itself much more with my personal limitations than with the subject in the subheading. There have been many Christian (and other) mystics, and, if I am to be consistent with what I have written in earlier chapters, I am bound to say that their writings must be taken seriously if we are to do justice to all the evidence on the basis of which we seek to understand the world. My difficulty is that I am not convinced that everyone is capable of being or becoming a mystic, and I also have philosophical difficulties with some of the language of mysticism. My position is that although I do not deny the importance of mystics and mysticism, I think that it represents a specialized branch of religious practice that is available to very few.

One of the great modern exponents of mysticism was the Anglican laywoman Evelyn Underhill (1875–1941), whose book *Practical Mysticism* was an attempt to commend mysticism to ordinary people.[8] She defined mysticism as

---

[8] E. Underhill, *Practical Mysticism: A Little Book for Normal People*, London: J. M. Dent & Sons, 1914. Cited here in the edition published by Eagle, Guildford, 1991.

the art of union with Reality. The mystic is a person who has attained that union in greater or lesser degree; or who aims at and believes in such attainment.[9]

The method of attaining such unity, if I understand the book correctly, involves a series of steps in which the individual strips from him- or herself anything and everything that obscures Reality. It involves detachment not only from worldly possessions but also from ways of seeing life that are bound up with personal priorities, ambitions and hopes. The various steps are described in the book, including three forms of contemplation. Underhill quotes frequently from the greatest exponents of mysticism, and shows convincingly how their insights agree, although they come from various times and countries. I have two problems with all this: the use of the term 'Reality' and the sense that mystical practice is a human striving after God; although to be fair to Underhill, she does quote writers who liken a passage from darkness to a kind of rebirth in which 'God's *action* takes the place of man's *activity*'.[10]

Because, philosophically, I think that abstract ideas are often merely words that need to be grounded in specific circumstances,[11] I can make no sense of the term 'Reality' when it is used on its own. Readers will recall the opening words of Chapter 1 above, that prayer is a word that is used in various ways. For 'Reality' to make any sense it has, for me, to be related to particular objects and circumstances; but when this is done there is the further problem of whether saying that something is real adds anything to what is being said about it.

---

[9] Underhill, *Mysticism*, p. 2.

[10] Underhill, *Mysticism*, p. 83.

[11] For example, I argue in my *Myth in Old Testament Interpretation* (Beihefte zur Zeitschrift für die Alttestamentliche Wissenschaft 134) Berlin: de Gruyter, 1974, that there is no such thing as 'myth' as opposed to 'myths', which are particular types of texts, and that 'myth' is a word that is used in different ways in different contexts.

The problem with the idea that mysticism is a human striving after God is that, as a biblical scholar, I see the movement in completely the opposite direction – not human striving after God, but divine striving after humans. I have already quoted 'You did not choose me, but I chose you' (John 15.16), to which could be added Paul's qualified statement in Galatians 4.9, 'but now ... you have come to know God, or rather to be known by God'. Moreover, the whole thrust of the Old Testament, not to mention the New, is about God taking the initiative in human redemption, a process that involves judgement as well as deliverance. What now follows cannot claim to be mysticism or a substitute for it, but only how attaining a goal of mysticism, the vision of God, appears to me to be possible.

A. J. Scott wrote that 'the humanity of Christ is that which translates the ineffable language of the Most High into men's native tongue'.[12] This statement both gives form and content to the otherwise incomprehensible God, and indicates that the primary movement is not from us to God, but from God to us. Accordingly, I would say that the quest (if that is the correct word) for the vision of God is begun, sustained, continued and ended in God's reaching out to us. It involves human effort, of course; but there is a paradox memorably and definitively described by Paul at 1 Corinthians 15.10:

> by the grace of God I am what I am, and his grace toward me was not in vain. On the contrary, I worked harder than any of them, though it was not I, but the grace of God which is with me.

I think of the Christian life as the quest to become ever more fully immersed in the stream of truth and life that issue

---

[12] A. J. Scott, 'On the Divine Will' in A. J. Scott, *Discourses*, London and Cambridge: Macmillan & Co., 1866, p. 16.

from God; or, to change the metaphor, the attempt so to hoist and adjust our sails, that the Spirit of God can fill them and take us where we need to be. In contrast to Underhill and the weight of mystical tradition that she represents, I see the task not as one of stripping away illusions so that we can approach Reality, but of allowing ourselves to be transformed by the initiative that God takes towards us. Both processes, of course, may involve similar disciplines and have some ends in common.

Prayers for the dead

There is nothing like the subject of prayers for the dead to arouse passions among churchgoers, and the subject often serves as a badge of churchmanship. While the very idea of praying for the dead is abhorrent to evangelicals, for whom the fate of the departed depends on how they responded in their life to the message about Jesus Christ, 'catholic' Christians deem it to be a mark of their catholicism that the departed are prayed for at the time of their decease, and very often on anniversaries of their death. The unexplained use of prayers for the departed is highly unsatisfactory, in my opinion. What is one asking God to do? This is rarely considered. Is the expectation that God will somehow be more merciful to the departed if they are mentioned at a service? We are very close to Phillips's 'the spell was not strong enough'.

The subject deserves to be explored here, because it may shed some light on how prayer can be understood. One of the most helpful discussions that I know dates from a time when the question of prayers for the departed had become a major issue in the Church of England. During the First World War the enormous loss of life of young men gave rise not only to requests from bereaved mothers and fiancées for forms of prayer for those killed in battle, but also to a change in practice in the Church. As G. K. A. Bell observed in his biography of Randall

Davidson, 'in 1914 such Prayers were most uncommon: by 1918 their use was widespread'.[13] Davidson, indeed, had been required by several bishops to justify the inclusion of the following prayer in Forms of Prayer issued by authority for use on 4 and 5 August 1917.

> We remember before thee our brethren who have laid down their lives in the cause wherein their King and country sent them. Grant that they, who have readily obeyed the calls of those to whom thou hast given authority on earth, may be accounted worthy of a place among thy faithful servants in the kingdom of heaven.[14]

The helpful comments that I want to discuss date from around the same time, in an essay in a book edited by B. H. Streeter.[15] The author of the essay was Lily Dougall, who wrote under the name of 'the author of "Pro Christo et Ecclesia"'.[16] The most important part of the essay is at the beginning in the form of a story. A woman came to a man for advice on praying for the departed. 'Are they not gone into God's keeping? Will He not do for them the utmost His power and love can do?' The man agreed that this was so, and the woman ceased to pray for the departed. Ten years later she returned, saying, 'All my life I have prayed for my friends on earth, but now I begin to realise that such prayer is futile and even an insult to God, for are we not all in His keeping? Will He not do for each one of us each day what is best and kindest?' The man agreed, and suggested that she should cease to pray for her friends. However, when she did this she felt miserable and said that she had lost the sense of God's blessing. The man replied,

---

[13] G. K. A. Bell, *Randall Davidson: Archbishop of Canterbury*, London: Oxford University Press, 3rd ed. 1952, p. 830, note 2.

[14] Bell, *Davidson*, pp. 828–9.

[15] B. H. Streeter (ed.), *Concerning Prayer: Its Nature, Its Difficulties and Its Value*, London: Macmillan & Co., 1917.

[16] 'Prayer for the Dead' in Streeter, *Prayer*, pp. 477–97.

Your distress proves that your prayers were acts of faith in God's love. Had they been the supplications of doubt, you would have been better off without them. When you prayed for your friends, the faith of your prayer each day opened a channel by which God's blessing could descend upon them and upon you. Begin again, and by your prayers enable God to give greater blessings to your friends upon earth, and also to those who have passed into the unseen, for we are all one family.[17]

The similarity with what was written in Chapter 3 above will be obvious. There, it was said that petitionary prayer was one of the ways in which God, working through us, was able to accomplish his purposes. The quotation above asserts the same point from a different perspective.

Whether or not readers of this book pray for the departed will be a matter of their personal choice. It is not something that I do myself, and I always feel uncomfortable in churches where it is done, because I do not know what the intention of the prayers is. However, I can see no difficulty in the practice if it is done in the spirit of the story told by Lily Dougall. If it was our practice to pray for our family and friends while they were alive, why should we stop once they die? If, during their lifetime, we commended them to a loving God, why should we not do so if we believe them to have entered God's nearer presence? In my own case I suspect that my reluctance to pray for the departed is motivated by a desire to avoid mediaeval ideas of purgatory, and the existence of chantries, where masses were said for the departed who were wealthy enough to found them and employ priests to staff them, the aim being to speed their passage through purgatory to paradise. I recognize that for this hideous past to cast such a strong shadow over my present thinking and practice is illogical and indefensible.

---

[17] 'Prayer for the Dead' in Streeter, *Prayer*, p. 480.

Questions for reflection and discussion

1 What biblical and other texts have you found particularly helpful in trying to affirm God's presence?

2 Do you agree that too much stress is sometimes laid on the need for congregations to be fed 'simple' faith?

3 In a recent television series five people were invited to embrace the discipline of silence for a week, in order to learn more about their souls. Was this a good idea or not?

4 Do you pray for departed friends and members of your family? If so, why? If not, why?

6

Praying with the Old Testament

———•·•·•———

Even regular churchgoers may be surprised to discover what rich resources there are in the Old Testament for a life of faith and prayer. The case for the Old Testament is seldom argued upon these lines, and must never be overlooked. It is not going too far to say that the Old Testament is indispensable for a Christian understanding of God and thus of prayer. In the section on Affirmation (p. 45) there were a number of references to the Old Testament. Psalm 23, in particular, provided passages that spoke powerfully of the abiding presence of God and of his support in time of need; and regular churchgoers will not be surprised that the psalms should be referred to in this connection. What is not so well known is that the narrative traditions of the Old Testament also provide rich resources for the life of faith and prayer, not to mention texts such as the book of Job. Such resources will be considered in the present chapter.

There is also a secondary aim of this chapter. It has become common recently to attack Christian faith by attacking the Old Testament, concentrating on passages that appear to display the alleged cruel and malevolent God of the Old Testament. These are well known and include the narratives about God inflicting plagues on the Egyptians as well as on the Israelites as they journey through the wilderness, and God's command to Joshua to destroy the Canaanite inhabitants of the Promised Land. That such attacks depend upon very limited use of what is actually contained in the Old Testament, as well as a superficial knowledge of its content and how to handle it, does not need to be argued here. A helpful discussion of the issues has recently been provided by Eryl Davies.[1] The whole matter appears in a very different light when the Old Testament is read from the perspective of the life of faith and of prayer.

The present chapter will concentrate upon two aspects of prayer not dealt with elsewhere in this book, and although one of them is also found in the New Testament, its occurrence there is greatly illuminated by what precedes in the Old Testament. The two aspects are prayer as strength in weakness, and prayer as argument with God.

Prayer as strength in weakness

In the Additions to the book of Esther, which can be found in the Apocrypha in Protestant Bibles and as part of the Old Testament text of Esther in Catholic Bibles, there is a moving and beautiful prayer prayed by Esther as she prepares to approach her husband, King Artaxerxes. She has learned of the plan of Haman to destroy the Jews living in the Persian empire and wishes to tell the king and to seek his help in frustrating the plan. To approach the king, however, is fraught with danger. One may do so safely only if specially invited. If uninvited, a suppliant must hope that the king will extend his golden sceptre as a sign of good will; otherwise, death may ensue (Esther 4.11). It is therefore with considerable trepidation that Esther approaches her task, and before she does this, she prays to God (Esther 14.3–19). She begins,

O my Lord, thou only art our King; help me, who am alone and have no helper than thee, for my danger is in my hand.

---

[1] E. W. Davies, *The Immoral Bible: Approaches to Biblical Ethics*, London: T. & T. Clark International, 2010.

She recalls the stories that formed her awareness of her people and their God, stories of God's mighty deeds for his people, but also of the people's waywardness. She continues,

> Remember, O Lord; make thyself known in this time of our affliction, and give me courage, O King of the gods and Master of all dominion! Put eloquent speech in my mouth before the lion, and turn his heart to hate the man who is fighting against us . . . help me, who am alone and have no helper but thee, O Lord.

Whatever the origins of this composition, and there is no need here to go into the very complicated textual history of the book of Esther and its Additions,[2] whoever wrote it had clearly experienced what many Christians know, that in times of difficulty a sincere admission of weakness and inadequacy before God can be a means by which God provides the strength to perform a task. In August 1998 I spent a month in Bad Endorf in Bavaria, Germany, looking after a small Lutheran congregation and its local health spa. Having arrived on a Saturday and taken the first services the next day, I was called out on that Sunday afternoon to a member of the Lutheran congregation who had just died. I found him surrounded on his death bed by his extended family, all of whom were Catholics, and I had no idea what Bavarian Catholics expected a priest to do in such circumstances. I had to rely entirely on my inadequacy and weakness and ask God to sustain me. Because the deceased had been a very important man in the mainly Catholic Bad Endorf, and the Lutheran church building was small, it was decided to hold the funeral service in the Catholic church. The whole village attended, and the church was packed. Again, it was only by relying on my weakness that I felt able to cope with conducting such a high-profile service in German in an unfamiliar

---

[2] For details see the article by C. A. Moore, 'Esther, Additions to' in *The Anchor Bible Dictionary*, New York: Doubleday, 1992, vol. 2, pp. 626–33.

environment. That has not been the only time when a recognition of weakness was the way in which God provided some kind of strength.

A similar kind of prayer to that of Esther is found in Genesis 32.9–12. Jacob, having defrauded and fled from his brother Esau, is returning to his native land after many years. This will entail a meeting with Esau. He prays to God ahead of this reunion:

> O God of my father Abraham and God of my father Isaac, O LORD who didst say to me, 'Return to your country and to your kindred, and I will do you good,' I am not worthy of the least of all the steadfast love and all the faithfulness which thou has shown to thy servant.

He recalls how God has blessed him materially, and prays as much for the safety of the family that accompanies him as for himself. The prayer expresses his weakness, probably for the first time in the way in which his character is portrayed in the Old Testament. It is followed by the mysterious incident in which Jacob wrestles with an angel, and prevails although being disabled. It has been said that this mysterious encounter is the answer to his prayer. Certainly, the Jacob who is now renamed as Israel is a humbler, weaker, character than the trickster of earlier narratives. At a deeper, spiritual level, the chapter (Genesis 32) may indicate that God can answer our prayers by making us weaker and therefore better able to draw upon his strength.

Feelings of inadequacy do not, however, always lead in Old Testament narratives to people's finding strength from God. There are two instances in which a person called to serve God tries to avoid the call by professing weakness and inadequacy. In Exodus 3 and 4, Moses gives several reasons why he should not be entrusted with the task of delivering his people from slavery in Egypt. First, he professes not to know the name of the God who is commissioning him. When this name has been disclosed to him, he insists that his message will not be believed by the people. God reassures Moses by enabling him to work signs, although these do not entirely satisfy him. His next excuse is that he is not an eloquent speaker. God deals with this objection by appointing Aaron to be his spokesman. A similar reluctance to accept a divine commission is found in the opening chapter of Jeremiah. In response to the word that comes to him from God saying that Jeremiah has been designated to be a prophet since before he was born, Jeremiah insists that he is only a youth. The Hebrew word used here, *na'ar*, can mean anything from a child only a few months old to a robust teenager. From the perspective of the Hebrew, however, what matters is the fact that it is not until riper years are attained that a person can credibly perform certain roles in the community. A Jewish saying dating from the end of the second century AD sets out the ages at which certain responsibilities can be undertaken, and only at the age of 30 can a person exercise authority.[3] Although this saying is 800 years later than the time of Jeremiah, it expresses a point of view that is found in many ancient and modern societies. Jeremiah's response, therefore, is an expression of weakness in the sense that he is being called to do something that nobody will take seriously, given his age.

Traditional interpretation of the Bible will take these incidents in the lives of Moses and Jeremiah to be the actual responses of historical persons. For modern critical scholarship the narratives are the product of the cultural memories of the ancient Hebrews, and this gives the stories a greater depth of meaning.[4] If we are dealing with an historical Moses and an historical Jeremiah, we have the responses of two individuals, and are

---

[3] Aboth 5.21 in H. Danby, *The Mishnah*, Oxford: Oxford University Press, 1933, p. 458.

[4] See further J. W. Rogerson, *A Theology of the Old Testament: Cultural Memory, Communication and Being Human*, London: SPCK, 2009.

none the worse for that. If we see the stories as expressions of cultural memories, we are tapping into a communal spirituality that had learned from long experience that to respond to the call of God was to embrace a costly discipleship, and that one of the resources for coping with the tasks demanded by that costly discipleship was a recognition of human weakness that made space for the working of the power of God. Indeed, the biblical stories of Moses and Jeremiah (probably more so in the case of Moses) show exactly what the cost of discipleship entails. Moses is initially rejected by the people he is sent to deliver from slavery (Exodus 5.21), and when the deliverance has been successfully achieved, he continues to face complaint and rebellion. Jeremiah's life is threatened (Jeremiah 20.10; 38.1–6) and, at the end of his life, he is mocked by men and women who say that the troubles that have come upon the people have come only because they have paid attention to Jeremiah's words (Jeremiah 44.15–19). Prayer as strength in weakness thus acquires an additional dimension. It is especially (but not exclusively) connected with the demands that come from entering the service of God, and the perils that such service may bring. It is God's way (but not the only way) of empowering those who try to serve him. The witness of the believing community in ancient Israel to the paradoxes involved in being called to serve God, finding this service costly, and gaining strength from the inability to do this without God, is a powerful illustration of the fact that God makes himself known to us, and is not something of human manufacture.

There are, of course, two obvious New Testament examples of the prayer of strength in weakness: the prayer of Jesus in the Garden of Gethsemane (Mark 14.36), and the prayer (although the actual words are not recorded) of Paul to be delivered from his 'thorn in the flesh' (2 Corinthians 12.7). In the latter case, Paul writes that he besought the Lord 'three times' (perhaps a way of saying 'many times') for relief from the ailment, or whatever it was.[5] The reply from God was, 'My grace is sufficient for you, for my power is made perfect in weakness' (2 Corinthians 12.9). This may or may not have been a new discovery for Paul; it is certainly clearly apparent in the Old Testament.

So far, narrative examples have been given of the 'strength in weakness' prayer; but a notable example of the strength in weakness prayer is Psalm 22. Not only does the psalm begin with the well-known complaint that God has forsaken the psalmist. As the psalm continues, a situation is revealed that suggests that both the psalmist and his enemies consider the psalmist to be close to death. The complaint that he is 'poured out like water' (Psalm 22.14) recalls the observation in 2 Samuel 14.14 that 'we must all die, we are like water spilt on the ground, which cannot be gathered up again'.[6] In verse 18, the psalmist's enemies are already dividing his clothes among themselves in anticipation of his speedy demise. Then, out of the gloom, there appears a ray of hope that transforms the psalm from lament into a hymn of praise. This is obscured in almost all translations of verse 21, but an impressive body of expert opinion is in favour of the translation,

> Deliver me from the mouth of the lion,
> And from the horns of the wild oxen.
>
> You have answered me![7]

In the moment of complete weakness, the psalmist finds strength, and can look to the future, not necessarily his future, with hope.

A slightly different form of the prayer of strength in weakness is one in which one person prays that another may find

---

[5] See the discussion in C. K. Barrett, *The Second Epistle to the Corinthians* (Black's New Testament Commentaries), London: A. & C. Black, 1973, pp. 314–16.

[6] See, further, J. Rogerson, *The Psalms in Daily Life*, London: SPCK, 2001, p. 6.

[7] See Rogerson, *A Theology of the Old Testament*, p. 148.

strength. A good example is 2 Kings 6.8–17. It concerns the power of the prophet Elisha to foresee the movements of the king of Syria and to advise the king of Israel accordingly. The king of Syria suspects a traitor in his court, but is advised that Elisha is the culprit. An expedition is therefore mounted by the king of Syria to apprehend Elisha, who is residing in Dothan, a town at the northern end of the hill-country of Ephraim, not far from where it joins the Valley of Jezreel. When Elisha's servant awakes in the morning he finds the town surrounded by the king of Syria's army. He is greatly distressed, and asks Elisha what can be done. Elisha assures him that 'those who are with us are more than those who are with them', and prays to God that his servant's eyes may be opened. This God does, and the servant sees that beyond the Syrian army are the armies of God. 'The mountain was full of horses and chariots of fire round about Elisha' (2 Kings 6.17).

It is necessary to repeat here what was said above about the responses of Moses and Jeremiah to God's call. We are not dealing with historical records of what once happened at Dothan in the ninth century BC. We have a cultural memory which is bringing to expression the communal experience of religious, perhaps prophetic, groups in ancient Israel that had learned that, against the odds, this tiny people could survive the threats posed to them by the superior, sometimes vastly superior, civilizations that surrounded them. In the light of the survival of the people, it was not an exaggeration to say that 'those who are with us are more than those who are with them', and it was appropriate to pray that others might be, or become, aware of this. It is also appropriate in today's world. What the Church calls the communion of saints is a vision of the 'great cloud of witnesses' (Hebrews 12.1) that surrounds struggling congregations, divided churches and perplexed individual believers. It is helpful to pray that God will open our eyes and the eyes of others so that in weakness we may view the present from the perspective of eternity.

Prayer as argument with God

This heading may surprise readers. Surely, we should not dare to argue with God! Yet this is what often occurs in the psalms when the psalmists complain about the prosperity of the wicked and the trials of trying to be faithful for God.[8] Indeed, it has long been recognized that what are called 'psalms of lament' constitute by far the greatest number of compositions to be found in the Psalter. The section about Psalm 22 above treated this psalm as an example of the prayer of strength in weakness. It could also be said that it is an example of a prayer as argument with God. After all, the psalmist begins by accusing God of having forsaken him. However, classifying psalms as 'psalms of lament' is not necessarily helpful to understanding them as prayers, as the present part of the chapter will try to demonstrate.

One of the best-known psalms of complaint is Psalm 73. The writer complains that those who treat God with contempt appear to prosper in the world and enjoy great popularity. The psalmist, who tries to take God seriously, does not prosper, and his efforts meet with derision from other people. The psalmist's dilemma is resolved when he goes to the temple and is granted a vision of what lies beyond the immediate present. The prosperity of the wicked is a temporary illusion and they will not escape retribution. The trouble with the psalm read in this way, and those like it that deal in different ways with the problem of the manifest unfairnesses of the world and the plight of those who try to be loyal to God, is that it reduces God to a factor in an intellectual discussion. In effect, these psalms are seen as intellectual arguments about the existence of God and how belief in God's existence can be squared with the presence of evil and wickedness. It is not being suggested

---

[8] See further Rogerson, *Psalms in Daily Life*.

here that this is an unimportant question; the issue is whether this is the correct way to interpret such psalms.

It is at this point that Psalm 22 becomes crucial. The complaint of the psalmist here is that he seems to have lost touch with God. While he complains also about those who taunt him and suggest that God has indeed abandoned him, he is not concerned with their fate or, indeed, with justifying himself before God. He feels just as distressed as if he had been let down by an earthly friend, and he goes out of his way to remind God of how intimate he felt his relationship with God to be.

> It was you who helped me burst from the womb,
> and laid me upon my mother's breasts.
> I have depended upon you since my birth,
> and you have been my God from my mother's womb.[9]

In the light of this, the dramatic change in tone in the psalm at verse 24 is understandable. The psalmist is somehow assured that God has not forsaken him, and he is able to respond to this with praise and thanksgiving.

Psalm 88 can be read in a similar way. This is the most negative psalm in the whole Psalter, with no ray of light at all.[10] On the face of it, the psalmist's complaint is that he has lost all hope in this life, and is facing death. However, it is arguable that this is a misreading of the psalm, and that the psalmist's problem is not that he fears losing his life, but that he fears losing his relationship with God. The psalmist thinks, mistakenly in the light of passages such as Psalm 139.8,[11] that God's power does not extend to Sheol, the place to which the departed go, according to Hebrew conceptions of existence after death.

---

[9] Psalm 22.9–10, translation in Rogerson, *Theology of the Old Testament*, p. 145.

[10] For a translation and discussion see Rogerson, *Theology of the Old Testament*, pp. 138–43.

[11] 'If I ascend to heaven, thou art there! If I make my bed in Sheol, thou art there!'

The psalmist is like someone having to say goodbye to a very close friend whom he may never see again. This is how he feels about God, and this is the ground of his complaint. If this is correct, it opens the way to how we can think about some of the psalms and use them to shed light on prayer as argument with God.

In my Old Testament Theology I have suggested that the way in which complaints are made against God in the psalms can only be done by people who stand in a very close relationship to him.[12] I have suggested the analogy of a high court judge who has teenage children who can say to him what no one else would dare say. While, in his court, he has power to imprison anyone who addresses him in abusive language, at home his children can express in no uncertain words what they think about him and his attitude to life. What they say is made possible only by the intimate relationship that they enjoy with him. If we take this analogy to the psalms of complaint, we can see and use them not as instances of intellectual discussions *about* God, but as expressions of an intimate relationship *with* God. Further, this intimate relationship is based upon absolute trust in the faithfulness of God, something expressed so sublimely in Psalm 23. We need to think more deeply about prayer as argument with God.

It has to be admitted that this will not be easy within the Christian tradition of prayer, although the Jewish tradition of prayer is quite familiar with the practice, simply because there are many instances of it in the Old Testament. In fact, some of the most notable examples come in narrative parts of the Old Testament. In Genesis 18.22–32, for example, Abraham argues with God about whether God would be justified in destroying Sodom if ten righteous persons could be found there. Abraham approaches God respectfully: 'Behold, I have taken upon myself

---

[12] Rogerson, *Theology of the Old Testament*, pp. 142–3.

to speak to the Lord, I who am but dust and ashes.' Nevertheless, he argues robustly, and is concerned to uphold the principle that the judge of all the earth should do what is right (Genesis 18.25). Similar instances of argument with God are found in the story of Moses. Reference has already been made to the attempt of Moses not to accept God's commission to lead the Hebrew people out of slavery. The dividing line between the prayer of strength in weakness and the prayer of argument with God is not always clear. In Numbers 14 Moses faces a crisis because ten of the spies who have been sent to spy out the Promised Land have brought back a very unfavourable report. The people, on hearing this, have considered choosing a leader who will take them back to Egypt, a proposal that displeases God, who threatens to strike the people with pestilence (Numbers 14.12). In this situation Moses has some hard words to say to God (Numbers 14.13–19). He says that if God does not bring the people to the Promised Land the Egyptians will conclude that God was not powerful enough to complete this task. He pleads with God to have mercy on the people and to continue to bear with them.

It is necessary to repeat what was said earlier in connection with the attempt of Moses and Jeremiah to evade the call of God. We are not dealing with actual historical people in historical situations. We are dealing with the cultural memory of spiritual realities, that are given expression in the form of stories. The speeches of Abraham and Moses that have just been outlined are examples of the narrative formulation of spiritual realities. They witness to the fact that in some circles in ancient Israel, groups or individuals enjoyed a certainty of the reality of God, an intimacy with him based upon absolute trust in his faithfulness, which enabled them to argue with him about the perplexities of life, and to find relief and strength as a result.

This section would not be complete without a reference to the book of Job, surely the supreme example in the whole of the Bible of prayer as argument with God. Job – whether we think of him as an individual whose personal experiences are the basis for the book, or whether he is a literary creation through which a community expresses its experiences – has to fight on two fronts. His so-called friends, who never, incidentally, address God personally in the book, defend the justice of God by trying to persuade Job that he must have committed a very grievous offence in view of the misfortunes that have come upon him. (According to the Prologue in chapters 1–2 he has lost all his property, and his immediate family has been killed, apart from his wife). Job's main concern, however, is to reconcile his misfortunes with his belief in God's fairness. He does not claim to be blameless, only that he has done nothing to deserve such overwhelming suffering. Unlike his friends, Job does address God personally. They speak *about* God; he speaks *to* God; and some of his statements exhibit the paradox of the prayer as argument with God, namely, that seemingly bitter things can be said out of a relationship of trust. Here is an example from chapter 7.

> I will not restrain my mouth;
> I will speak in the anguish of my spirit;
> I will complain in the bitterness of my soul.
> Am I the sea, or a sea-monster,
> that thou settest a guard over me?
> . . .
> Why hast thou made me thy mark?
> Why have I become a burden to thee?
> Why dost thou not pardon my transgression
> and take away my iniquity?[13]

Yet at 13.15 Job can declare, 'though he slay me, yet will I hope in him', and whatever difficulties there may be in translating Job 19.25–26 (the passage whose traditional rendering begins,

---

[13] Job 7.11–12, 20–21.

'I know that my Redeemer lives'), it can be taken as an assured minimum that Job, who earlier in chapter 19 has spoken about his alienation from his extended family, asserts that God himself will stand by him as his *go'el*, his kinsman, whose duty it is to uphold his honour.[14] At the end of the book, God reproves the friends who had devoted so much effort to defending him and commends Job who had argued with and against him. 'The Lord said to Eliphaz the Temanite: "My wrath is kindled against you and against your two friends; for you have not spoken of me what is right, as my servant Job has"' (Job 42.7). This statement only makes sense in the context of the prayer as argument with God.

What this means in practice is that in reading and using the Bible, we should try to be aware of prayer as argument with God. There is a wonderful example in Jeremiah 20.7 where Jeremiah, in effect, accuses God of having deceived him into becoming a prophet.[15] Approaching the Bible in this way will throw new light on a number of passages.

How might this affect the way that we pray? The headings under which different types of prayer are classified – adoration, confession, intercession – do not usually include the heading 'argument'. Perhaps this is why it is not easy to conceive of this type of prayer in Christian tradition. Once we admit it, and become aware of its deep roots in the Old Testament, we may find that to practise it is to be enriched. We may find that complaining to God, about what we consider to be his shortcomings or his failures to address injustices, not only relieves our frustrations, but actually brings us closer to God. It is certainly something worthy of serious consideration.

---

[14] The translation of Job 13.15 is complicated by the fact that while the Hebrew text has *lo'* meaning 'not', an ancient tradition reads the text as *lo* meaning 'to him'. The translation given above follows the alternative *lo* 'to him' and takes the Hebrew to mean literally 'if he kills me, to him (i.e. in him) will I hope'.

[15] See Rogerson, *Theology of the Old Testament*, p. 149.

Questions for reflection and discussion

1 Recall or discuss an occasion on which you found strength in weakness. How did it occur, and what did it teach you about yourself and about God?

2 Do you find the idea of arguing with God helpful, or alarming, or both?

3 Are you surprised by the depth of resources available in the Old Testament for a life of faith and prayer?

7

The Lord's Prayer

———•◆•———

When I was a student I came to know a Brethren family living
in south London. They were so open that they arranged for me
to be invited to take a Sunday evening service at their Gospel
Hall. There was one strict condition, however: under no circumstances was I to use or mention the Lord's Prayer. If I did, some
of the less 'open' members present would be offended, and some
might even learn the unpleasant truth that I was not only an
Anglican, but training to be ordained.[1] The objection to the
Lord's Prayer was that its recital in the services of mainstream
churches amounted to the 'vain repetitions' condemned by Jesus
in Matthew 6.7. It is difficult not to sympathize with this point
of view. It is possible to explain, liturgically, why the Lord's
Prayer occurs twice in the main traditional Anglican services,
once with and once without the doxology. In the communion
service of the Book of Common Prayer, for example, the Lord's
Prayer without the doxology, said by the priest alone at the
beginning of the service, is the remains of the private devotions
of the celebrant before the service. The Lord's Prayer after communion is the response of the congregation to what they have
received, and the addition of the doxology here follows ancient
liturgical practice. Liturgical justification can also be given for
the double occurrence of the Lord's Prayer at morning and

---

[1] Not only do the Brethren not have ordained clergy, but the founder of the movement, J. N. Darby, considered the notion of a clergyman to be a dispensational sin
against the Holy Spirit.

evening prayer. However, congregations are not usually aware of these liturgical niceties. So far as their experience of worship is concerned, they are expected to recite the Lord's Prayer at least once, and sometimes twice, when they attend divine worship. The result is that the prayer becomes so familiar that it is almost treated with contempt. I remember hearing a version of the Lord's Prayer made up entirely of place names near London, one of whose purposes was to point out how easy it was to rattle off the prayer without thinking of its meaning. Apparently, there are several versions. The one I heard ended, 'for thine is the Kingston, the Purley, the Crawley, for Edgware and Edgware. Amen'.

How can the Lord's Prayer be made special? How can we remember that it is the *Lord*'s Prayer? In many parts of Germany it is the custom to ring a bell during the service when the Lord's Prayer is recited. Whether this helps German worshippers to treat the Lord's Prayer as something special, I do not know, but it is a custom that I would like to see widely adopted. Another way in which its special nature might be realized is by giving it an eschatological interpretation, that is, following Ernst Lohmeyer, by seeing it as the prayer which Jesus gave to his disciples to equip them for the crisis that was coming upon them in his life, death and resurrection.[2] This is the approach that will be taken here.

The original form/s of the Lord's Prayer

The prayer has been handed down to us in two versions, in Matthew 6.9–13 and Luke 11.2–4. The version in Luke is shorter than that in Matthew, something obscured in the Authorized Version of the Bible, which used a Greek text in which the shorter, unfamiliar, version in Luke had been expanded into the longer, familiar version in Matthew, which

---

[2] E. Lohmeyer, *The Lord's Prayer* (1952), London: Collins, 1965.

was (and is) used in worship. In the Revised Standard Version the two forms of the prayer are as follows.

Matthew 6.9–13

Our Father who art in heaven,
Hallowed be thy name.
Thy kingdom come,
Thy will be done,
On earth as it is in heaven.
Give us this day our daily bread;
And forgive us our debts,
As we also have forgiven our debtors;

And lead us not into temptation,
But deliver us from evil.

Luke 11.2–4

Father,
hallowed be thy name.
Thy kingdom come.

Give us each day our daily bread;
And forgive us our sins, for we ourselves
forgive every one who is indebted to us;
And lead us not into temptation.

The doxology, 'For thine is the kingdom . . .' is present only in later manuscripts of the New Testament, although the *Didache*, an early Christian text dating from perhaps AD 100, has a version of the prayer very similar to that in Matthew, and with a slightly shortened form of the doxology.

That there are two forms of the Lord's Prayer can be explained in several ways. Jesus may have taught the prayer in a longer or a shorter form; or the longer form may be an elaboration of the shorter form, deriving either from Jesus or from his followers. Most scholars think that the Lukan form is closest to what Jesus taught and that the form in Matthew is an expansion to make explicit what is implicit in the shorter form. Certainly, the form in Matthew does not add anything to what is already in Luke. Jesus would have taught the prayer in Aramaic, and various scholarly attempts to reconstruct the Aramaic have been made.[3] Scholars also point out that the Greek version in the New Testament may well come from a single line of tradition, because the Greek word translated as 'daily' in the phrase about daily bread is not otherwise known in the whole of Greek literature. The Prayer will now be considered phrase by phrase, as found in the shorter version in Luke.

Father

When I began to teach in Durham in 1964 the thing that I found most difficult was not delivering my first lecture (scary stories were told of lecturers who had read their first lecture, realized that it had taken only twenty minutes, and had then read it again!) but being expected to call my colleagues by their first names. I had made an overnight transition from being a student to being a lecturer. I had only very recently called my teachers 'Sir', and although I had not studied in Durham, I was familiar with the scholarly work of several of those who were now my colleagues, and I held this work in great esteem. I was now being treated as an equal by these scholars, and was expected to call them by their first names. I found this very difficult.

There must be many walks of life in which social or academic distinctions have been maintained by the need for people to be addressed in a respectful way. One thinks of the

---

[3] Examples can be found in Lohmeyer, *Lord's Prayer*, pp. 27–9; E. Lohse, *Vater Unser: Das Gebet der Christen*, Darmstadt: Wissenschaftliche Buchgesellschaft, 2nd ed. 2010, pp. 13–14.

medical profession, for example, and the titles used in hospitals. When I was ordained in 1964 bishops expected to be addressed as 'My lord'. The current usage of Bishop Fred or Bishop Jim was unimaginable. When I began teaching I addressed my students as Mr Smith or Miss Jones, and they called me 'Sir'. This began to change in the 1970s, and by the time I left Durham to go to Sheffield, I had begun to address my students by their first names, even though they continued to call me 'Sir'.

These observations are an introduction to the astonishing fact that the Lord's Prayer begins with the form of address 'Father'. In the Old Testament, surprisingly, God is rarely addressed as 'Father'.[4] This form of address had become more common by the time of Jesus, usually as *'âvînu*, the Hebrew for 'our Father'. Jesus, however, in his own prayers used the Aramaic *Abba*. This is clear from the prayer in the Garden of Gethsemane, where the Gospel tradition transliterates the Aramaic *Abba* before giving the Greek equivalent, 'Father'. There has been debate over whether *Abba* meant 'Daddy'; but whether it did or not, it was an informal address to God not usually used in prayers of the time. Because of the special and unique nature of the relationship between Jesus and God it is not, perhaps, surprising that Jesus had such an unusual way of addressing God. What is striking, however, is that he wanted his followers to use the same form of address; and we have evidence from the letters of Paul that the early Church did use this form. In Romans 8.15–16 Paul writes, 'When we cry, "Abba! Father!" it is the Spirit himself bearing witness with our spirit that we are children of God.' At Galatians 4.6 he writes, 'God has sent the Spirit of his Son into our hearts, crying, "Abba! Father!"' Incidentally, these references to *Abba* in Paul may be evidence for the use of the Lord's Prayer in the churches known

---

[4] One of the rare examples can be found at Isaiah 63.16.

to Paul. C. K. Barrett, in his commentary on Romans, notes that 'it [the use of *Abba*] corresponds exactly to the opening of the Lord's Prayer in the Lucan form (Luke xi.2), and Paul's reference here may be to the use of this prayer in Christian worship'.[5]

Assuming that what was in order for the first followers of Jesus is in order for us, what right do we have to address God in such an informal way? The answer is 'none at all!' If anything, we should feel far, far more embarrassed about this than I felt about calling my colleagues by their first names when I began to teach in Durham. How dare we approach the Creator of the universe, the King of the Kings of Kings, the Holy One, blessed be He (as a Jewish form of address puts it) in any way other than one of awe and wonder? The example of Abraham in Genesis 18.27 is instructive here: 'Behold, I have taken upon myself to speak to the Lord, I who am but dust and ashes.' But just as it was my colleagues in Durham who wanted me to use their first names, so, astonishingly, according to Jesus, it is God who wants us to address him informally. My colleagues wanted this because of the special relationship that existed among members of the theology department in Durham. God wants us to do this because he wishes to establish a special relationship with us, mind-blowing though this thought may be. In a way, the whole of the gospel is contained in this word Father, for it implies the establishment of a special relationship between a God of unimaginable power and splendour, and human creatures characterized by transience, selfishness, ignorance, arrogance and wickedness. Such a relationship can only be established from the God-ward side. It was effected ultimately (although anticipated and partially realized in the Old Testament) by the ministry and death of Jesus.

---

[5] C. K. Barrett, *The Epistle to the Romans* (Black's New Testament Commentaries), London: A. & C. Black, 1962, pp. 163–4.

In the form of the Lord's Prayer used by the churches in worship, the words employed come from Matthew, 'Our Father'. It is likely that this is an expansion of the original Abba, Father: first, to make it conform to words common in Jewish worship of the time of Jesus; second, perhaps, to soften the outrageous implication that we can or should address God in such an informal way. But it is only if we find ways of recovering how special and remarkable the Lord's Prayer is, and develop corresponding ways of using it, that we shall begin to do justice to its remarkable opening, and all that that implies. The addition or expansion in Matthew, 'which art in heaven' strengthens the paradox. We are invited to use an informal mode of address to one whose dimension of being is that of heaven.

Hallowed be thy name

The word 'hallowed' is not one that we use in common speech today, with the exception of the name 'Halloween', which is short for 'All Hallows Eve' – 'All Hallows' being an alternative name for All Saints Day. The latter festival falls on 1 November, and All Saints or All Hallows Eve is the day before, 31 October. 'To hallow' therefore means something like 'make holy', and 'hallowed' as an adjective means something like 'sacred' or 'holy'. 'Hallowed be thy name' means something like 'may your name be sacred, or be made holy'. The most obvious way of understanding this is to regard it as a prayer for God's name to be treated with respect, and that is something which is earnestly to be desired, especially in view of the current popularity of the exclamation 'Oh my God!' This was something that Jewish tradition took, and takes very seriously. The command not to take the name of the LORD in vain (Exodus 20.7) was applied so strictly in the Judaism of the time of Jesus that it was an offence, punishable by stoning to death, to pronounce the special name of God, whose consonants in Hebrew were YHWH. As an indication of how seriously the matter is taken today by observant Jews, I possess books in English by orthodox Jews in which the word God is spelled 'G-d' and books in Hebrew in which the Hebrew word for God, *elohim*, is spelled *eloqim*.

However, because reverence for the name of God was so widely observed in the time of Jesus, it can be argued that 'hallowed be thy name' had a different meaning in the Lord's Prayer, and that it meant something like 'act in such a way that your power will be manifested in the world, and people will acknowledge the sanctity of your name and being'. If this is correct, has this prayer been answered in the sense of being acted upon by God, or is it something that is prayed for in hope?

It was once said that the ministry of Jesus was the answer to the Lord's Prayer.[6] If this is so, then God indeed manifested his power in response to the petition, although not in the way that human expectations would have wished. However, we must never forget that Christianity is a remarkable phenomenon, given that it began with the absurd proclamation by a small group of men and women that a man publicly executed for insurrection was the Servant chosen by God to bring salvation to the world. To those who view the ministry and death of Jesus through the eyes of faith, he was indeed the way chosen by God to hallow his name. The ministry of Jesus changed the history of the world and the way that we think about God, and did so in a way that emphasized the importance of non-violence and self-giving suffering love, for all that the Church has betrayed this vision on many occasions. When we pray, 'hallowed be thy name', whatever else we are doing, we are affirming God's unique way of making his power and presence known, and are asking that he will continue to do so.

---

[6] I heard this from a student in Manchester who was asked to discuss the quotation in an examination in June 1958, which had been set by T. W. Manson before his death in the May of the same year. Whether this was original to Manson I do not know. I seem to have come across a similar sentiment in Lohmeyer, but cannot locate the passage!

Thy kingdom come

The discovery that the theme of the kingdom of God was central to the teaching of Jesus played an important part in my journey into faith. It was a discovery in the sense that my contacts with Christianity through school assemblies and church parades had given no indication of how central the kingdom of God was in Christian faith. When I began to take a greater interest in Christianity, and heard sermons in 'evangelical' churches, the sermons seemed mostly to be about 'The Lord Jesus Christ' and his sacrifice on the cross. Rarely was the teaching of Jesus addressed. I remember agreeing heartily with the comment of Leslie Weatherhead that 'the creeds of the Church do not once mention the phrase which, more than any other, was on the lips of Jesus', and that 'The Thirty-nine articles elaborate doctrines about which Christ said nothing, but they are silent about the main theme of all his words.'[7] It was also from Weatherhead that I came across the definition of the kingdom as a 'Kingdom of right relationships'.[8]

Becoming interested in the kingdom of God meant becoming acquainted with the teaching of Jesus, most of which in the first three Gospels is about the kingdom of God. The parables present the kingdom in intriguing ways. It is likened to a man stumbling accidentally across treasure buried in a field, or a merchant dealing in pearls suddenly coming across a pearl so exquisite that he feels compelled to sell all that he has in order to possess it. It is likened to various types of growth: to a mustard seed, to a seed growing secretly, to a sower sowing his seed broadcast. It is likened to a great banquet; it has a social dimension in the parable of the Labourers in the Vineyard, where all the workers gain the same wage regardless of how

[7] L. D. Weatherhead, *In Quest of a Kingdom*, London: Hodder & Stoughton, 1943, p. 41.
[8] Weatherhead, *Quest*, p. 39 referring to G. R. H. Shafto, *The Stories of the Kingdom*, London: SCM Press, 1922, p. 37.

many hours they worked. It is the proximity of the kingdom that the disciples are commissioned to preach when they are sent out on their missionary journeys. It is something that people are invited to enter, not in some future existence, but here and now.

Becoming interested in the kingdom also meant becoming acquainted with the scholarly debates then raging about whether Jesus expected it to arrive in the immediate future, whether it had already arrived almost without remainder, or whether it was present in the ministry of Jesus, established by his death and resurrection, and due to be consummated at the end of time. I remember being struck by a quotation from Rudolf Otto that appeared in C. H. Dodd's *The Parables of the Kingdom*, 'not Jesus brings the Kingdom, but the Kingdom brings him with it'.[9] The importance of this quotation was and is that the kingdom of God is a way of speaking about God's rule in the world. This rule is already established, so far as human response is concerned, in the calling of Israel to be a kingdom and priests unto God (Exodus 19.6). In the ministry of Jesus it has drawn near, as God has taken the initiative in establishing his rule in a new way, a way that involves his self-disclosure in and through Jesus. For me, learning about the kingdom and seeking to enter it and serve it meant finding a centre to my life that had been lacking previously, and which made sense not only of 'ordinary life' but of the exalted moments which I experienced especially though my interest in music. Whatever else the kingdom was about, it afforded glimpses of itself in all that in human experience and the world of nature was noble, pure, uplifting and challenging. As embodied in the life and teaching of Jesus, it assumed a form that made it possible to become a way of life for anyone drawn to serve it.

---

[9] C. H. Dodd, *The Parables of the Kingdom*, London: Nisbet & Co., 1936 (rev. ed.), p. 45 note 1, citing R. Otto, *Reich Gottes und Menschensohn: ein religionsgeschichtlicher Versuch*, Munich: Beck, 1934, p. 80.

What are we doing when we pray 'thy kingdom come'? We are praying that God's will may be done on earth as it is in heaven, to cite what is probably in Matthew's tradition an ancient expansion and spelling-out of the simple petition that is found in Luke. We are acknowledging that God's kingdom is already present in the world, having been begun in the Old Testament and having been decisively established in the ministry, death and exaltation of Jesus. But we are also acknowledging the paradox that God's kingdom is far from having been realized in the world; that each generation has to be confronted anew by its message, to either accept or reject it. We are praying that our present world will come to know of the kingdom, acknowledge its presence, and seek to realize it in personal, social and political relationships. We are also praying about the future, thereby expressing our hopes for a better world and a better humanity to go with it. We are committing ourselves to a task that is beyond our capabilities, but which demands our total engagement. In this regard, our use of the petition may not be too far removed from that of the first disciples of Jesus, who were commissioned to proclaim a kingdom that had come, was coming and was to come.

Give us this day our daily bread

This is one of the most difficult parts of the Lord's Prayer to understand and to pray meaningfully, for two reasons. First, it is arguably trivial if all that it amounts to is a request for us to receive on a daily basis the food that we need for our sustenance. Admittedly, this is a very 'Western' and affluent point of view. There are no doubt many parts of the world where a prayer for daily sustenance will never be trivial; but how can the petition be meaningful in parts of the world where obesity, not malnutrition, is the more urgent problem? The second reason is that the Greek word translated as 'daily' occurs nowhere else in Greek literature as known to us, and is therefore of uncertain meaning. Four main theories, based upon arguments about the

Greek word, have been put forward.[10] The first, which connects the Greek word with a word for 'substance', yielding 'substantial bread', enabled the Church to link the petition with the provision of the eucharist. The second theory, following the same line, took 'substantial bread' to mean bread necessary for human sustenance. The third approach took the word to denote bread needed for today, i.e. 'daily bread', which is probably how most users of the prayer understand the petition. The fourth approach took the petition to mean 'give us today tomorrow's bread'. Luz argues that the fourth view is the most likely from the linguistic point of view, and to this it can be added that it gives an eschatological or anticipatory sense that is in accord with the idea that the Lord's Prayer is given to the disciples to help them face the crisis that is precipitated by the coming of the kingdom of God in the ministry of Jesus.

In the New Testament the kingdom of God in its heavenly and consummated form is described in terms of a heavenly banquet (Matthew 22.1–14), and the petition 'give us today tomorrow's bread' could therefore be a request for a foretaste here and now of that which was yet to come. This line of interpretation has further possibilities if we think that the fellowship meals that Jesus had with his disciples and others, including the Feeding of the Five Thousand and the Last Supper, were meant to be anticipations of the heavenly banquet, and thus tangible enactments of the presence of the kingdom here and now. Further, although linguistically the petition probably cannot be linked with the eucharist, such a link is possible if we think that the eucharist was and is meant to be an anticipation of the heavenly banquet.

How all this can be condensed into a simple explanation of the meaning of the petition about the provision of bread, I am

---

[10] See U. Luz, *Das Evangelium nach Matthäus* (Evangelisch-Katholischer Kommentar zum Neuen Testament I/1), Zürich: Benzinger Verlag; Neukirchen-Vluyn: Neukirchener Verlag, 1985, pp. 345–6.

not sure. What it perhaps indicates is that the Lord's Prayer is something that needs to be meditated upon, and not just chanted automatically.

Forgive us our sins, for we ourselves forgive every one who is indebted to us

In the fourth petition of the Lord's Prayer there is one significant difference between the version in Matthew and that in Luke. Anyone who is familiar with the Book of Common Prayer version of the petition: 'and forgive us our trespasses, as we forgive them that trespass against us' and attends a service in which the Lord's Prayer is recited according to the Authorized Version of Matthew 6.9–13 will be surprised to hear other worshippers saying, 'and forgive us our debts, as we forgive our debtors' (Matthew 6.12). The Prayer Book 'trespasses' appears to reflect the tradition of English Bible translation going back to Tyndale, who used 'trespasses' at Matthew 6.12 while the Authorized Version more accurately translated the Greek *ofeilémata* as 'debts'.[11] 'Trespasses' (or sins) represents what appears at Luke 11.4 where the Greek is *hamartiai*. There is obviously a big difference between 'debts' and 'sins', although it is striking that Jesus used the analogy of debts to illustrate aspects of sin and forgiveness. Experts who have sought for the Aramaic word spoken by Jesus have suggested *hov* (with a hard initial 'h' as in English 'huge'), a word that hovers between sin, debt, guilt and obligation, and which could easily have been taken as 'debt' by the Matthew tradition and 'sin' by the tradition underlying Luke.[12] This opens up wide possibilities of interpretation, but in the first instance the matter of sin and forgiveness will be considered.

---

[11] The Geneva Version of 1560 also has 'dettes' (*sic*).

[12] Lohse, *Vater Unser*, p. 14; M. Jastrow, *Dictionary of Talmud Babli, Yerushalmi, Midrashic Literature and Targumim*, New York: Pardes, 1950, p. 429.

The petition for forgiveness is a reminder that those who pray the Lord's Prayer come before God as sinners who need to rely on his mercy. The astonishing fact that such people are also invited to address God intimately as 'Father' is, by implication, emphasized. However, God's forgiveness is dependent upon human willingness to forgive, not in the sense that God makes this a strict condition, but because humans who cannot forgive other humans lack the capacity to conceive of God's mercy. This kind of blindness is well illustrated by the parable of the Unforgiving Servant in Matthew 18.23–36, in which a servant is forgiven the debt of a colossal sum of money by his master, the equivalent of 15 years' wages for a day labourer, and who then refuses to forgive a fellow servant who owes him a day's wage, but has him cast into prison for the debt. The point is well made by the petition in the Lord's Prayer that the kingdom of God has practical and social aspects; that it is not a cosy relationship with God that is isolated from interpersonal relationships. If the kingdom of God is a kingdom of right relationships, it means that those who are disciples of the kingdom are committed to being peacemakers. In the Sermon on the Mount, Jesus enlarges on this aspect of the petition by insisting that his followers must forgive their enemies and those who persecute them (Matthew 5.43–44). The kingdom may well provoke opposition and persecution. The disciple of the kingdom must not respond in like manner. From the perspective of hindsight, this petition points to the cross, where Jesus prays for those who are crucifying him (Luke 23.34).

If the sense of the Aramaic *hov* as obligation is followed up (see above) there is another possibility of interpretation. We are all obliged to others in various ways, especially to our parents and teachers, and others who have guided and inspired us in our journeys through life. In most cases, we can never repay what we call these debts directly. Our parents and teachers may well be dead. Even if our teachers are still alive, in what way can we repay them? The most likely possibility is that we try to use what we learned from them in such a way that they would feel that their efforts on our behalf had not been wasted. I would like to think that the man who taught me German at secondary school would be pleased to know that very many years later I read and use German in my work almost every day. Readers will be able to add many examples from their own experience. One way, then, in which it would be legitimate to enlarge on the fourth petition of the Lord's Prayer would be to paraphrase it as follows: 'help us to repay the debts of gratitude that we owe to others'. We can never, of course, repay the debt of gratitude that we owe to God, but can only ask him to take us as we are and use us in spite of our inadequacies.

Lead us not into temptation

A straightforward interpretation of these words implies that God leads people into temptation (however that is understood) and that the petition asks him not to do this. This is surely problematic. If God does lead us into temptation, this is either for our own good, in which case we should not be praying for God to desist from doing it, or because of some malicious streak in God, which hardly accords with the teaching of Jesus that God does not play tricks on people (see Matthew 7.9–11; Luke 11.11–13). Even if 'temptation' is understood as 'testing', and the story of God's testing of Abraham in Genesis 22 by ordering him to sacrifice his son Isaac is cited (compare also John 6.6), we are still faced with the question of whether we should want to avoid what God commands or devises. The book of Proverbs has positive things to say about God's testing of those he loves (Proverbs 3.11–12).

A radical alternative way of interpreting the words has been proposed by Lohmeyer.[13] For him, 'temptation' is not something that assails individuals but is 'the final encounter between God

---

[13] Lohmeyer, *Lord's Prayer*, pp. 203–8.

and (the) evil (one) which ushers in God's kingdom'.[14] However, this encounter is not something that happened in the past (although it did in the victorious confrontation of Jesus of the 'principalities and powers' on the cross). It happens in the present, in which the disciples of Jesus manifest and represent the kingdom in a world that is not yet fully redeemed, and in which they bear the brunt of the attempt of the powers of evil to usurp and confound the will of God. The disciples of the kingdom are called upon to engage in a struggle that is beyond their human capabilities, but in which they can rely upon the grace and strength of God. The petition 'lead us not into temptation' is in this context a recognition of the unequal task to which disciples of the kingdom are called, and is a way of drawing on the strength which God supplies. In 1971, when the Church of England issued its Alternative Services Series 3, the translation of the Lord's Prayer offered the words 'do not bring us to the time of trial'. Whether or not this was an attempt to capture something of the 'eschatological' interpretation of the petition I do not know. It did not prove to be popular, and *The Alternative Service Book* of 1980 reverted to the familiar 'lead us not into temptation'.

Can this line of interpretation be justified? Luz, whose judgement is always balanced and authoritative, thinks not.[15] He argues that there is no precedent for the Greek word translated as 'temptation' to refer to an eschatological event. However, he defines 'temptation' as something behind which the powers of evil stand, and in commenting on the addition to, or enlargement of, the petition that comes in Matthew, 'but deliver us from evil', defines evil not in terms of the evil one (i.e. the devil, as many Christian interpreters have done) but as powers of evil such as illness, oppression, wickedness. In some ways, this is not so far from what Lohmeyer is saying, with this difference.

---

[14] Lohmeyer, *Lord's Prayer*, p. 206.
[15] Luz, *Matthäus*, pp. 348–9.

If Luz is correct, the emphasis is more upon the desire of the individual or community to be freed from the effects of the evil that can assail anyone or a group of people in the kind of world in which we live. It is an affirmation of the sovereignty of God in such a world, despite evidence to the contrary. If Lohmeyer is correct, the petition is less for protection from the assaults of what is evil, and more for strength to bear these assaults, in the belief that the disciples of the kingdom, in confronting such assaults, are helping the kingdom to be manifest in the world. A possible way of putting this into English would be 'sustain us in the time of trial'.

Conclusion

How should we pray the Lord's Prayer? It is not the purpose of the present chapter to prescribe how this should be done, apart from saying that however else it is used it should not be gabbled frequently and thoughtlessly. It seems to me that we have to decide between two possibilities. The first is that it is a 'general purpose' prayer, applicable to all situations, in which we acknowledge our dependence upon God for our daily needs and upon his forgiveness for our demeanours, and in which we ask that our lives will pass in tranquillity and peace, spared from the vicissitudes that might afflict us. The second is that the Lord's Prayer is about the crisis caused by the coming of the kingdom, and that it is to be used by disciples of the kingdom as they seek to proclaim and live out the implications of its coming. The first approach suggests tranquillity, the second suggests crisis. We must make our own choice. It will be clear from what I have written in this chapter what choice I have made.

Questions for reflection and discussion

1 Do you agree that the Lord's Prayer has become too familiar, and therefore virtually meaningless? In what ways could we try to make it special?

2 Do you find it helpful to think of the Lord's Prayer as something given by Jesus to help the disciples cope with the crisis brought by his ministry? Can this also apply to Christians today?

3 'Do not bring us to the time of trial.' Is there a need for a radical modern translation of the Lord's Prayer, or do you prefer the traditional form(s), provided that the meaning of the clauses is explored in sermons/discussion groups?

Epilogue: when prayer is difficult or impossible

————— ·•·•· —————

It is not often that I find it difficult or impossible to pray, but it is certainly something that happens to me from time to time, and it may well be that others have had the same experience. In his biography of Cardinal Basil Hume, Anthony Howard relates that the Cardinal found it difficult to pray during his last illness and that he had to content himself with holding a crucifix and reflecting on Christ's sufferings.[1] If this was true for a Benedictine monk who had spent much of his life in prayer, there may certainly be some hope and encouragement for those of us much further down the scale of devotional practice. Certainly, when I had some unexpected heart trouble in the autumn of 2008, and before a pacemaker was fitted to deal with it, I had some difficult times with regard to prayer, especially when I was admitted to hospital after some bad turns during a weekend. The other occasions when I have found it difficult to pray are when everything seems to have gone wrong and there has been one frustration after another.

An experience that perhaps resembles this in the Bible is that attributed to Jeremiah in his so-called confessions. Jeremiah 20.9 reads,

> If I say, 'I will not mention him, or speak any more in his name,' there is in my heart as it were a burning fire shut up in my bones, and I am weary with holding it in, and I cannot.

---

[1] A. Howard, *Basil Hume: The Monk Cardinal*, London: Headline, 2005, p. 310.

The context implies that Jeremiah is reluctant to speak in God's name because this only brings threats against his life. When he is thus silent, however, he finds within him a burning fire, presumably to speak out, which he cannot contain. The part of this outburst with which I can identify is not that I find within myself a burning fire that I cannot contain, but that I find a dissatisfaction that can only be resolved when I resume my prayers, such as they are. In this I am helped by several considerations.

First, there is that part of the parable of the Prodigal Son that has been called the parable of the Waiting Father. If the father in the parable was prepared to wait for a long period for his son to return from the far country, I can be assured that God will wait to hear my prayers when I resume them after a break. Second, I am emboldened by a passage that occurs in Lamentations 3. In the midst of a dark meditation on the punishments inflicted upon his people by God because of their unfaithfulness, the clouds suddenly break and there is a shaft of brilliant light.

> The steadfast love of the LORD never ceases,
> his mercies never come to an end;
> they are new every morning;
> great is thy faithfulness.

It comes as no surprise that these words have inspired a number of hymns. Not only are there the English hymns 'New every morning is the love' and 'Great is thy faithfulness'; there is also the much-loved German hymn 'All Morgen ist ganz frisch und neu, des Herren Gnad und grosse Treu' ('The Lord's grace and faithfulness are fresh and new each morning'). Indeed, the knowledge of these words is not only something that can be used in affirmation; they are also part of the armoury of a Christian when faced with situations that make prayer difficult or impossible. They are encouragements to return to prayer as soon as is possible. I have also found that it is helpful to remember words that are not only useful prayers in good times, but which help in bad ones. I recently came across the following German prayer, to which I add a free translation.

> In den Tiefen, die kein Trost erreicht, lass doch deine
> Treue mich erreichen.
> In den Nächten, wo der Glaube weicht, lass nicht deine
> Gnade von mir weichen.
> Wenn ich deine Hand nicht fassen kann, nimm die
> meine du in deine Hände.
> Nimm dich meine Seele gnädig an,
> Führe mich zu einem guten Ende.   (Justus Delbrück)[2]

> In the depths no comfort reaches, let your mercy still
> embrace me.
> In the nights when faith is weak, do not let your grace
> towards me weaken.
> When I cannot grasp your hand, let my hand be grasped
> by yours.
> Graciously receive my soul,
> lead me to a perfect ending.

I am not sure whether it is right to feel guilty when it becomes hard or impossible to pray. Obviously, ceasing to pray is not a trivial matter; but guilt can sometimes have the effect of making it more difficult to resume what we are guilty about not doing. Perhaps the positive thing about this is that it reminds us of our frailties and of the astonishing fact that it is with such creatures as ourselves that God delights to have contact through the manifold channels that we call prayer.

---

[2] J. Delbrück in H. Gollwitzer et al. (eds.), *Du hast mich heimgesucht bei Nacht: Abschiedsbriefe und Aufzeichnungen des Widerstandes 1933–1945*, Munich: Kaiser Verlag, 1954, p. 103.

Bibliography

Barrett, C. K., *The Epistle to the Romans* (Black's New Testament Commentaries), London: A. & C. Black, 1962

Barrett, C. K., *The Second Epistle to the Corinthians* (Black's New Testament Commentaries), London: A. & C. Black, 1973

Belden, A. D., *The Practice of Prayer*, London: Rockliff, 1954

Bell, G. K. A., *Randall Davidson: Archbishop of Canterbury*, London: Oxford University Press, 3rd ed., 1952

Bonhoeffer, D., *Widerstand und Ergebung: Briefe und Aufzeichnungen aus der Haft*, Munich: Kaiser Verlag, 1951; ET *Letters and Papers from Prison*, London: SCM Press, 1953

Bultmann, R., 'The New Testament and Mythology' in H. W. Bartsch (ed.), *Kerygma and Myth*, vol. 1, London: SPCK, 1953, pp. 1–44

Crowder, C., 'Otto's *The Idea of the Holy* revisited' in S. C. Barton (ed.), *Holiness Past and Present*, London: T. & T. Clark, 2003, pp. 22–47

Dalferth, I. U., and H. Von Sass (eds.), *The Contemplative Spirit: D. Z. Phillips on Religion and the Limits of Philosophy* (Religion in Philosophy and Theology 49), Tübingen: Mohr Siebeck, 2010

Danby, H., *The Mishnah*, Oxford: Oxford University Press, 1933

Davies, E. W., *The Immoral Bible: Approaches to Biblical Ethics*, London: T. & T. Clark International, 2010

Delbrück, J. in H. Gollwitzer et al. (eds.), *Du hast mich heimgesucht bei Nacht: Abschiedsbriefe und Aufzeichnungen des Widerstandes 1933–1945*, Munich: Kaiser Verlag, 1954

Dodd, C. H., *The Parables of the Kingdom*, London: Nisbet & Co., (rev. ed.) 1936

Dougall, L., 'Prayer for the Dead' in B. H. Streeter (ed.), *Concerning Prayer: Its Nature, Its Difficulties and Its Value*, London, Macmillan & Co., 1917, pp. 477–97

Edwards, J. R., 'Lohmeyer, Ernst (1890–1946)' in D. K. McKim (ed.), *Dictionary of Major Biblical Interpreters*, Nottingham: Inter-Varsity Press, 2007, pp. 671–5

Grouchy, J. W. de (ed.), *The Cambridge Companion to Dietrich Bonhoeffer*, Cambridge: Cambridge University Press, 1999

Hammann, K., *Rudolf Bultmann: Eine Biographie*, Tübingen: Mohr Siebeck, 2009

Howard, A., *Basil Hume: The Monk Cardinal*, London: Headline, 2005

Jastrow, M., *Dictionary of Talmud Babli, Yerushalmi, Midrashic Literature and Targumim*, New York: Pardes, 1950

Kelly, G. B., 'Prayer and Action for Justice: Bonhoeffer's Spirituality' in J. W. de Grouchy (ed.), *The Cambridge Companion to Dietrich Bonhoeffer*, Cambridge: Cambridge University Press, 1999, pp. 246–68

Köhn, A., *Der Neutestamentler Ernst Lohmeyer: Studien zu Biographie und Theologie* (Wissenschaftliche Untersuchungen zum Neuen Testament 2. Reihe 180), Tübingen: Mohr Siebeck, 2004

Lawrence, Brother (Nicolas Herman), *The Practice of the Presence of God: The Best Rule of a Holy Life Being Conversations and Letters of Brother Lawrence*, London: Epworth Press, (no date)

Lohmeyer, E., *The Lord's Prayer*, London: Collins, 1965

Lohse, E., *Vater Unser: Das Gebet der Christen*, Darmstadt: Wissenschaftliche Buchgesellschaft, 2nd ed. 2010

Luz, U., *Das Evangelium nach Matthäus* (Evangelisch-Katholischer Kommentar zum Neuen Testament I/1), Zürich: Benzinger Verlag; Neukirchen-Vluyn: Neukirchener Verlag, 1985

Magee, J. B., *Reality and Prayer*, London: Hodder and Stoughton, 1958

Manson, T. W., 'The Sayings of Jesus' in H. D. A. Major, T. W. Manson and C. J. Wright, *The Mission and Message of Jesus: An Exposition of the Gospels in the Light of Modern Research*, London: Ivor Nicholson and Watson, 1937, pp. 301–639

Mary Clare SLG, Mother, *Learning to Pray*, Oxford: SLG Press, 2nd ed. 2006

Moore, C. A., 'Esther, Additions to' in *The Anchor Bible Dictionary*, New York: Doubleday, 1992, vol. 2, pp. 626–33

Otto, R., *Reich Gottes und Menschensohn: ein religionsgeschichtlicher Versuch*, Munich: Beck, 1934

Otto, R., *Das Heilige: Über das Irrationale in der Idee des Göttlichen und sein Verhältnis zum Rationalen*, Munich, C. H. Beck, 1917, 25th ed. 1936. ET *The Idea of the Holy: An Inquiry into the Non-rational Factor in the Idea of the Divine and its Relation to the Rational*, Harmondsworth: Penguin, 1959

Quick, O. C., *The Realism of Christ's Parables*, London: SCM Press, 1937

Phillips, D. Z., *The Concept of Prayer*, Oxford: Blackwell, 1981

Rogerson, J. W., *Myth in Old Testament Interpretation* (Beihefte zur Zeitschrift für die Alttestamentliche Wissenschaft 134), Berlin: de Gruyter, 1974

Rogerson, J. W., 'The Old Testament View of Nature: Some Preliminary Questions', *Oudtestamentische Studiën* 20 (1977), pp. 67–84

Rogerson, J., *The Psalms in Daily Life*, London: SPCK, 2001

Rogerson, J. W., *A Theology of the Old Testament: Cultural Memory, Communication and Being Human*, London: SPCK, 2009

Saas, H. von, *Sprachspiele des Glaubens: Eine Studie zur kontemplativen Religionsphilosophie von Dewi Z. Phillips mit ständiger Rücksicht auf Ludwig Wittgenstein* (Religion in Philosophy and Theology 47), Tübingen: Mohr Siebeck, 2010

Schottroff, L., 'Die Güte Gottes und die Solidarität von Menschen: Das Gleichnis von den Arbeitern im Weinberg' in L. Schottroff, *Befreiungserfahrungen: Studien zur Sozialgeschichte des Neuen Testaments*, Munich: Kaiser Verlag, 1990, pp. 36–56

Scott, A. J., 'On the Divine Will' in A. J. Scott, *Discourses*, London and Cambridge: Macmillan & Co., 1866

Selby, P., 'Christianity in a World Come of Age' in J. W. de Grouchy (ed.), *The Cambridge Companion to Dietrich Bonhoeffer*, Cambridge: Cambridge University Press, 1999, pp. 226–45

Shafto, G. R. H., *The Stories of the Kingdom*, London: SCM Press, 1922

Streeter, B. H. (ed.), *Concerning Prayer: Its Nature, Its Difficulties and Its Value*, London, Macmillan & Co., 1917

Underhill, E., *Practical Mysticism: A Little Book for Normal People*, London: J. M. Dent & Sons, 1914; reprint Guildford: Eagle, 1991

Weatherhead, L. D., *A Shepherd Remembers: A Devotional Study of the Twenty-Third Psalm*, London: Hodder and Stoughton, 1937.

Weatherhead, L. D., *In Quest of a Kingdom*, London: Hodder & Stoughton, 1943

Weatherhead, L. D., *A Private House of Prayer*, London: Hodder and Stoughton, 1958

Wildberger, H., *Jesaja 1–12* (Biblischer Kommentar Altes Testament), Neukirchen-Vluyn: Neukirchener Verlag, 1972

Wittgenstein, L., *Philosophical Investigations* (trans. G. E. M. Anscombe), Oxford: Blackwell, 1953

Wittgenstein, L. *Philosophische Untersuchungen, Kritisch-genetische Edition* (ed. J. Schulte et al.). Darmstadt: Wissenschaftliche Buchgesellschaft, 2001

Index of biblical references

Index of names and subjects